Sam and Me
&
the Hard Pear Tree

Sam and Me
&
the Hard Pear Tree

Jami Yeats-Kastner

First published by Jacana Media (Pty) Ltd in 2014

10 Orange Street
Sunnyside
Auckland Park 2092
South Africa
+2711 628 3200
www.jacana.co.za

ISBN 978-1-4314-2023-0

Cover design by publicide
Set in Sabon 11/15pt
Printed and bound by Creda Communications
Job no. 002239

See a complete list of Jacana titles at www.jacana.co.za

This book is dedicated to my long-suffering hubby and our beautiful boys. All three of them.

It isn't just on nature's whim
That we grow our children from within;
It isn't just mere luck or chance
Which children join us in life's dance.

It's one great knowing,
One great search
Launched within the universe
Until we find where we belong,
The ones that need us, make us strong.
Before this time, beyond this space,
You met in a celestial place
And that is how you came to be
The five of you, a family.

Jackie Yeats-Du Preez

This book is about so much more than a tree, obviously. It's about how my son Sam sent me a message from the other side, using all his power to make the message strong enough to be captured in this physical world. And that is what finally gave me the courage to share it.

Have you ever felt something you couldn't quite name that sparked a feeling of recognition and made your heart rejoice? Once you have felt that, the knowing is always inside you. Sometimes it's a booming voice and sometimes a distant echo, but it's always there. I have felt it for about two years now. When Sam left, though, I allowed that voice in completely. It sang to me, comforted me and tried its best to drown out my own screams.

Six months after The Day It Happened I went for a walk. My kinesiologist M had told me that the hard pear tree would help with my grief, so I set out to find it in the ancient forest called Platbos, not far from our farm in the Western Cape. When I came upon it, I felt an urgent need to give it a hug.

Back at home afterwards, my friend C showed me the photo she had taken of me and the tree. And there you were, Sam, a soft purple light holding me, surrounding me, loving me.

And so the path began to unfold. It took a lot of courage to post that photo on Facebook. Firstly, it showed that I believe in angels. Secondly, it showed me *hugging a tree*! If someone had told me three years ago that I would be hugging trees and studying crystals I would have guffawed in their face. But things have changed. I have changed.

I was sure people would think I was crazy, but it was immediately obvious that this wasn't the case. The photo, and what it spoke of, resonated with so many. The next day I started my blog Crazybutterflylady. My first entry was based on this same picture. Now here you are, reading this book of Sam's messages. And that, dear reader, is no coincidence.

9 February 2014

It's a glorious day. I am sitting on the porch of my lovely new home with a cup of tea, looking out over our farm to the mountains beyond. The house is not quite finished, with only a concrete slab where the spare room should be. But for us, for our little family, it is perfect.

This journal started exactly a year ago. Yesterday was the first anniversary of the day that changed our lives forever, the day that shattered everything we thought we knew.

I am a 39-year-old mother, and life has been both cruel and kind to me. I have known blessings and joy and unimaginable sadness. I am a mother who has lost a child.

But I cannot let this define me, or define our family. We cannot allow sadness to be the overwhelming theme of our lives. So I choose joy, and this year has taught me that you do have a choice.

I thought – although I consider myself a strong woman – that if I ever lost a child my life would be over. I think we all feel like that, us parents. Yet when it happened, my grief allowed me to absolutely feel and understand the beauty of the universe and the infinite love that surrounds us all.

We will miss Sam forever and grieve for what he could have been here on earth. But his purpose was so big that it couldn't be accomplished in this world, you see. This is our path, the one we must walk together, as hard as it may be.

Sometimes you need to be completely broken to find the most powerful part of yourself.

I have three sons. Jack is six, tall, blue-eyed, gorgeous and sensitive with undiagnosed global developmental delay. Alex is four, athletic, highly intelligent and pretty hard-headed. Sam is a forever-perfect eighteen-month-old with the most amazing grin and brave, friendly nature.

In February 2013, a gloriously warm summer afternoon turned suddenly into a nightmare from which there was no escape and no respite. That is where this story begins. But it also begins long before that, and is a story that will never end.

In this last year I have found faith: faith that Sam is still with us; faith that death is not the end; faith in the kindness of strangers; and faith in myself and the strength of our family. I have learnt that love truly can survive the separation between this world and the next.

So we need to go back there, back to a year ago, the beginning of the end and the end of the beginning. It is twelve months yesterday since you left, Sam. A year, a lifetime, a second. My life is different now in so many ways and on so many levels.

I am not the only one out there. There are many of us walking around, going about our days, doing our shopping, hanging up the washing, pretending that we are whole people. Some are the walking wounded and some are the walking dead. We will forever be part of a club to which none of us wants to belong, and nothing anyone can say will change that.

But my heart is genuinely healing; the raw gaping wound is filling up with strength and hope. It is my wish that through sharing my path daily, I can help you walk yours.

9 February 2013

Yesterday my world ended.

I am strong, and I will get through this. Please God, I am strong, help me get through this. I don't want to remember the details, but I have to, and I have to learn to live with them. There was a lot of screaming, mostly coming from me. A lot of shouting, 'No, no, no!' and breaking of things. I threw myself onto my bed and screamed and cursed. Alex came into the room and he looked so scared. I tried to stop sobbing and said to him, 'Mommy's hurt her foot.' *Fucking come and take him away!* I wanted to shout, but everyone was either on the phone to paramedics or at the pool trying to revive Sam. I could hear the beeping of machines through my bedroom window and the sound of my husband's desperate CPR. He did everything right, but how do I convince him of that? I cracked and he coped, and I'm so proud of him.

Occasionally the CPR was interrupted by a wail or a scream of 'Come back, Sam!' From my own bed I screamed and screamed to cover the terrible sound of my husband's pain. I knew Sam was gone. When the ambulance took him away there was still the tiniest sign of life. But I knew from the first scream that my baby was gone.

Tragedy befalls us all in one way or another. But it's universally accepted, I think, that there is no greater pain than this. How do I process this? Where do I go when it gets too big?

My boys need me now, and they need my strength. In order to

survive this I have to find meaning in it. Aside from the absolute joy he brought us for nineteen short months, this can't be the end, surely? Sam was born with a great purpose, and I have to figure out what that is. He is happy and safe and smiling on me. I must say this to myself a thousand times a day. Look out for signs that he is around me. They will come, and they will comfort me.

Already the town of Stanford, recently so at war with itself, is standing together. Is this part of your purpose, Sam? Is this part of your plan?

Sam, I will honour you, my son. I will do whatever I must to ensure that your short life's purpose is fulfilled. Of course you know that for a long time now I have felt the need to somehow help special needs children. I saw the signs that this would be the right thing for me. You and I, my baby Sam, my brilliant, smiley, tireless boy, are going to start a charity. And my sisters, my friends, and everyone who loved you will help. I think maybe a learning centre or a school in Stanford that caters to children with special needs. You and I, my boy, are going to do so much good. And your name, and your purpose, will never be forgotten.

I just opened the door to another delivery. This one with the most beautiful chilli plants for your memorial garden. Do you see, Sam, how much power you wield? From a girl I haven't seen in twenty years who was somehow touched by you. Such a big, beautiful spirit you must have to inspire such an outpouring of love.

11 February 2013

Yesterday I had a very sad morning. Or mourning, as it were. I cried and I sobbed, read some of my love messages and then had a bath in some colour therapy oils (to make me a strong mother, this particular blend; highly recommended). And I asked Sam to send me a sign. In fact, I asked him to send me a butterfly. I knew I shouldn't, because it was too much to ask. It wouldn't happen, and then what? More despair? But sweet Jesus, it did! Peter is the one who pointed it out, and his obvious excitement surely means that he is starting to feel Sam too. It even sat on my hand, and my heart nearly exploded with joy.

I don't think everyone is lucky enough to receive such a clear message, but if we open our hearts and our eyes, maybe the signs are all around us. Yet you never know when, like this evening, the simplest thing can break your fragile peace. I was dishing pasta for the boys, and I suddenly became acutely aware that there were two bowls, not three. There was Jack's blue bowl and next to it Alex's red bowl. But where was the third? Where was my third? It's been three for so long. Three little bowls of pasta, three little bowls of cereal, three little sets of pyjamas laid out after bath time. And suddenly I remember that I will never use that third bowl again, and Jesus Christ it cracks my heart right open.

But I have to go on. I just do. I've heard too many stories from people who lost a sibling. 'My parents were never the same again.' That won't happen to us. Our home will be a happy one.

We will be present as parents and we will be happy. We must be.

In 2007 I painted a picture. A severely crap painting, as even those who love me would agree. It was of two stick figures with a little stick figure on the side holding his daddy's hand – me, hubby and Jack. In September 2009 I realised something was missing, and I painted a huge belly onto my stick-figure self to include the second child on his way. Now, in February 2013, it remained unchanged. So many times I had looked at that picture in the kids' room and thought, *I must add Sam to that.* And for some god-awful, got-too-busy, life-too-stressful reason I never had. But today I got out some paints my friend P had sent me (a very thoughtful present for a grieving person) and painted a big yellow butterfly above our heads. The very doing of it gave me great joy.

Poor Alex, the curious little creature. He was so angry today, so furious and defiant. I asked him why and he said, 'I'm just very cross.' Then we hugged and he said, 'Mommy, nothing must happen to you,' very quietly, right against my chest, almost afraid to speak the words. 'When are we all going to go there?' 'Go where?' I asked, though I knew what he was asking. 'To Heaven,' his tiny voice answered, desperate for reassurance, desperate for some kind of answer (aren't we all). In the best way I know, I gave him what he needed, the best I could from the bottom of my broken mommy-heart.

Funny how life works, isn't it? The whole esoteric journey I have been on for the past ten months, the whole spiritual search and growth I have experienced... I thought it was about getting out of the black hole I had found myself in. But it wasn't. It was to prepare me for the darkness I didn't even know lay ahead.

11 pm
Finally, exhausted from tossing and turning as I listen to the gentle snores of my family around me, I have given up on sleep. Sleep, my one true escape, and tonight it eludes me. So I sit here and write the long hours away.

And what of Jack, you may ask? How is my sensitive little soul handling all of this? The truth is, not very well. At five years old he understands plenty. In fact, he understands things in a way even I probably don't grasp. Being unable to express his grief in words must feel like such a lonely place. He coughs and sticks his fingers down his throat and tells me, 'I sick, I very sick.' Somehow I know that his words are simply stuck inside, as they have always been, and to him perhaps it feels like a sort of blockage in his throat. His face contorts as he struggles to get the words out, with sheer panic in his eyes when he gets really stuck and the word simply won't come. Breathe, Jack, slow down. Breathe. I use the sign language therapists have taught me, a visual tool to help Jack understand and take it in. Breathe. Such a simple instruction, such a natural act, yet such a difficult thing for my darling boy. It breaks my heart every single time. It's not okay to see him like this, it's not okay *at all*. But how do I help him? It's time to start the tutoring again.

Sam, you're now stronger than I am. Maybe you always were. You are infinitely powerful, and I ask you to help your brothers through their grief, and to help Jack to keep improving and be genuinely happy. Is that a lot of pressure? Not for a superhero it's not.

I was supposed to visit friends in Somerset West tomorrow, about an hour and a half's drive. I was really looking forward to seeing them – good friends, girlfriends. But I realise I will have to cancel. It's the strangest thing, this grief. You really don't know how you'll feel until you get there, hour by torturous hour. Today I was strong, and tomorrow I'll try my best to be strong. But tonight I am very, very weak. And that's okay too. But not while you're going through it. My heart is very, very, very, very, very sore.

When I pray now, I talk to Sam. It's him I ask to give me courage and strength. I've prayed quite a bit during the last ten months, but I've never known who exactly to address these monologues to. They always opened with something along the lines of 'Dear umm, Universe. No, God, sir, erm...' and then I would launch directly into a chat with the Almighty – the best name I came up with in the end, though it still never really fitted.

Tears are running down my cheeks as I write this, tears totally beyond my control. So I will try to write the tears down, and see if that helps. I miss you Sam, my darling boy, every single second of every single day. I miss you hard.

There, that feels a bit better. Tomorrow morning at 8 o'clock I am going walking on the farm with some of my thank-God-for-them friends. Then a group of us are having a garden planning meeting – for Sam's garden. It will be the most magical place in the world. For Sam's memorial service, we asked everyone to bring along a tree or a plant for his garden. We have so many plants and flowers that the front lawn looks like a nursery. And neighbouring farmers have offered compost, equipment and labour.

We are so incredibly blessed by the goodness and support from those all around us. But to be fair, I suppose we have been kind to many of them. This is one of the LGTs (life's great truths) I've discovered. People are nicer to you if you are nice to them first. If you try to be kind as much as possible, you will have many friends. Some will question your motives or take advantage of your kindness, but these people will naturally fall out of your life. Sometimes it's not possible to be nice. Under extreme circumstances some bitchiness is excused, nay, even encouraged. No need to be a doormat, but try to keep this to a minimum by first investigating whether the situation demands it, and then go balls to the wall. But gratuitous bitchiness is unnecessary and very bad karma.

Our garden will have trees, magic spots and secret sayings. He loves the outdoors, our Sam. And he will always be in this garden. The boys will help, of course, and they can put their own secrets and surprises in the garden. Not everyone is able to build a garden as a memorial. I am very blessed in that sense, I know. But I do think it will help me to heal if I can physically build some kind of monument to my beautiful child. Another LGT, while we're on the subject: try not to judge. Note I say 'try'. This does not mean I don't judge people. It simply means I try not to. Who gives a shit if someone lost all their money, smokes a joint once a day or believes in fairies? More power to them, I say. Just don't beat up your wife, hurt kids, steal from innocent folks or do stuff like that. It's okay to judge those people.

I have been pretty much hoping – and trying – to avoid the typical seven stages of grief. Frankly, they don't sound like much fun, and they loom in my future like great, terrifying clouds. I went through many of them with the Jack thing, and it was such a long, hard road. But with this, with Sam, I suspect I will have to go through each and every one. I guess that's why they say 'hour by hour'. The thought of an endless future without Sam is too big for me right now. But I can do the next couple of hours, I think. Tonight I am alone with my grief, and that is good, but hard. Tomorrow I will surround myself with people who love me again, and they will make me strong. I want very much to write about Sam, to tell you about him in every excruciatingly beautiful detail. But I am not ready yet. As the words come into my head they turn to tears before they can reach my pen.

I have such a lovely husband, you know. We bicker a lot, mostly about whose turn it is to feed the kids, why my credit card is maxed out, who forgot to put the chicken back in the oven so that the dog ate it – that sort of thing. But when the chips are down, we really love each other very deeply. And more importantly, we really like each other. If I could choose anyone at all to travel with or party with or lie on the couch with, it would be him. And I guess that's what makes our marriage work.

I can also tell you a bit about our other two boys.

Alex is my darling, impossible, loving, middle child. The poor kid at the moment doesn't know if he's coming or going. First, he was the second child with an older brother. As they grew, it became clear to him (and to us all) that he also needed to be Jack's big brother. And then along came you, Sam, and suddenly he was no longer the youngest. At first, he was far more reluctant than Jack to accept you. And then he grew to love you so intensely, and he became super-protective. Especially around water, oddly enough. He would panic and nearly cry if you went near the pool. 'Mommeeeeee!' he would shout, tugging at your arm. 'Put Baby Sam's wings on!' It's almost as if Alex knew on some level. Maybe we all know our life scripts, but forget. Is it easier for children to remember? Your brothers always called you Baby Sam, and I guess now they forever will.

Anyway, Alex is ridiculously cute, which is why he gets away with murder, I suspect. He's not as tall as Jack was at the same age, but perfectly built with wide shoulders, a skinny waist and a perfect little round bum. He reminds me of a Russian gymnast or a tightly coiled spring. My hubby calls him the short wheelbase Land Rover, all muscle and power and energy. He has shaggy brown hair which is always hanging in his eyes, because trying to give him a haircut is like wrestling with a piece of spaghetti. His eyes are not straight blue like his brothers, but blue with green rings around the iris, much like my own father. And, man alive, is he wilful. 'No, Mommy!' he will shout at me. 'I wanna make the rules. Why can't I make the rules?' Why indeed, my young Alex? Why can't we?

Let me tell you a bit about Jack.

When Jack was four months old, I took him for a check-up. Like most new parents, I suspect, I was not taking him so much to be checked as for the doctor to admire him and pronounce him perfect. Alas, it was not to be. Her words hit me like a wall of icy water. I could see she was worried, and I didn't like it one bit. When she finished the check-up, she wrote down the name of a paediatric neurologist. I knew somehow that her words were the end of something, of the dream all parents dream of their child being healthy and 'normal'.

God, I hate that word.

Anyway, that particular doctor was just the first rung on a

ladder that turned out to be high and steep. Doctors, neurologists, geneticists... pah, I've seen 'em all. I'm no stranger to a CT scan or an MRI, and all too familiar with the sound of my baby crying his heart out while people stick needles into him. Yet not one solid answer did I get. The gist was that he had severe low muscle tone. Now, for those who don't know and haven't spent hundreds of sleepless hours researching the Internet, low muscle tone is not considered a diagnosis, but a sign of an underlying condition or syndrome. You'd think with today's technology they would surely be able to find the reason, give you an answer, and let you get one solid night's sleep. But the world of syndromes, it turns out, is vast. The list of possible things your child could be suffering from is endless. No-one knows the cause, so there's no diagnosis, and therefore no prognosis.

Not a soul who hasn't loved a child with special needs will understand. My search was obsessive. Every new syndrome you find out about is terrifying, yet you can't stop researching. The need to put this problem in a box, label it and then deal with it accordingly is unmanageable. But there is no box for Sprog 1. God love him, he is the sweetest little thing. Not a mean bone in his body. But for some reason his muscles are weak and his brain works slightly differently from mine. Now you must believe me, I would not change a hair on this lad's head. And some of you will judge me when I tell you it's very hard. But judge away, people, judge away. I am too old and too selfish to care. Perhaps it's best summed up in some letters I wrote in March 2012 at my therapist's request. These letters were to be addressed to my Jack, to try to cope with my feelings. I tried to be honest in the first one, and not a word of it is a lie. Then I showed it to Sensible Sister, and she saw right through it.

'But isn't it hard for you? Don't you think you should say something about that?' So I sat down and wrote draft two of the letter. I thought I would feel disloyal writing it, but I didn't. I felt liberated. Here are these self-same letters, for your perusal and quite possible disapproval.

Letter to my darling son Jack, draft one:

There is a lot I need to say. I will never have enough time to say it all. But the most important thing, Jack, is that I love you. You are not what I expected. You are not what planned. But I would never, *never* change a single hair on your head. When you were four months old I took you for your first check-up. I didn't expect any surprises, and to me you were perfect. You still are. But the doctor diagnosed low muscle tone, and recommended we see a paediatric neurologist. It started us on a long and difficult path: from specialist to specialist, therapist to therapist, to hospitals and universities for blood tests and MRIs. Each result came back negative.

With the relief I felt at every syndrome ruled out came an equal measure of frustration. What could I call it? How could I help you if I didn't know what I was dealing with? And every doctor had, in different words, the same advice. 'There is clearly a problem, but we don't know what it is. We'll just have to wait and see how he develops.' Fine for them to say! So on and on we went, searching for the answer.

Then one day it dawned on me. I know why they can't find a diagnosis. Because there isn't one. There is nothing wrong with you. You are a pure and special being whose brain works a bit differently from mine. Your very Jackness is the reason why everyone who meets you loves you. And that is that. My obsessive Internet research stopped, and I finally accepted and saw the real you.

I now know that the universe sent you to me for a very special reason, and that there were some lessons I needed to learn. You have taught me patience. Not everything in life runs smoothly. Not everything in life will go exactly according to plan. I've always rushed through things in life, always in a hurry. But sometimes the best thing is taking your time to enjoy the moment, the gradual unfolding of a gift, fully appreciating each layer as it opens.

You have taught me not to care what others think or say, as that has no effect on your life. I used to worry a lot about what others thought, and at first, when it became clear that you were different from some of the other kids, I felt a small sense of embarrassment. Can you believe it? It seems like a lifetime ago. How could I feel embarrassed about having the most gorgeous, sweetest and most gentle child, just because he couldn't yet walk when others his age did? I now know how to be braver in my own life. I say what I think and I mean what I say, and I make no excuses for myself anymore. And that is because you came into my life. You taught me to appreciate the little things. While other mothers simply clapped when their child walked for the first time, watching you take two steps was the greatest moment in my life. My heart felt so full and so proud that I thought it might burst, and for days afterwards I walked around in a bubble of happiness that something others take for granted could bring us both such joy.

Every time I try to speak to friends about your latest magnificent achievement, such as saying, 'My name is Jack,' they try to listen but their eyes are blank. They will never know the joy I feel in my heart when you proudly show me a new skill. Your brave and independent spirit has shown me the value of perseverance. When I watch you coming downstairs on your own, it takes every ounce of my strength to not reach up to you and grab your hand. But I see the determination in the set of your mouth and the concentration in your every step, and I want to cry with happiness. And when you reach the bottom and shout, 'Well done, Jack,' I laugh with you at your achievement. And I see something in your eyes, Jack – the fighting spirit of a boy with something big to offer the world. You may struggle to communicate now, and I know that frustrates you. But there is something special about you. Something great lies in your future, and I can't wait to see what it is.

Letter to my darling son Jack, draft two:

There is a lot I need to say. I will never have enough time to say it all. But the most important thing, Jack, is that I love you. You are not what I expected. You are not what planned. But I would never, *never* change a single hair on your head. But God, it is frustrating being your mom. The way you constantly don't look where you are going and then wipe out. It's scary, man, and I can't let you out of my sight because of it. And the way you won't listen and just keep doing the same thing over and over. Is this part of your condition, or is it just naughtiness? Do I punish you if it's not even really in your control? And the need to grab things and squeeze things. Is it naughtiness, or something to do with the way the cream feels on your hands that appeals to you? And when you absentmindedly smack your brother on the back and cause a huge fight, is it because you can't communicate and that's how you get attention? Your total lack of understanding drives me mad sometimes. Do you hear me when I call you? Or is your mind somewhere else? *Do you hear me?* It's hard, you understand. And then your pure and gentle nature just blows my mind. But how long will it be this way? Yes, I see improvements every day, but how far can you go? It's *so* tiring having to lift you in and out of things, and carry you when you get tired. And I find it so hard to leave you with other kids, because I don't know how you'll cope. Will they be mean to you? Where does that leave me, Jack? How will I ever let you go enough to really enjoy parenting as I should? Or will there always be this constant worry, this constant anxiety? And all the extra work involved, the therapies, the planning, and now the diet. It's just so much. And the years of research and Internet searches, and the very real financial implications of it all. And I never know with you. The world is so full of danger for you. Or is it? It's hard enough being a mother and a parent, does it really have to be *this* hard? And I do get angry at you, and I guess maybe a tiny part of me gets resentful. And I do sometimes wish it was different, who wouldn't?

But God I love you. xxxx

A few days after writing the second letter to Jack, in one of my sporadic early attempts to keep a journal, I recorded the following.

Today I have made the decision to really fight for my boy. And also to fight for the other two, who are no less valuable nor precious because they are not Jack. It was the most difficult parenting day I have yet faced. As I write this, Jack is busy smacking me continuously on the shoulder shouting, 'Not! Not! Didn't!' What does it mean? Dunno, but this could go on for some time.

I'm alone at home since hubby has escaped to the sanctuary of the office, and the children are like sharks who smell blood in the water. They know I'm alone. There's only one of me and three of them, and all of them need me with every fibre of their being. They all clamber on me, cry, shout and go hysterical. Underneath it all I try to keep my cool, but the day has already been a long one, and it takes all my strength not to explode.

Today was Jack's third day at his new private pre-primary school. First day, great. Second day, not so good. Mutterings among the teachers about not being able to handle him without a full-time tutor to accompany him. This news is like an axe in my chest. So he will not be mainschooled? Is this really his future, to be an outsider and different his whole life?

The answer is one of the most frightening realisations I've ever had. Yes, he will be an outsider in this one-sided, blindfolded world we live in. And, yes, he will be different. Always. Is this perhaps easier for him to live with than for me?

Today it was terrible to watch Jack welcoming friends to his home, stretching out his hand to be shaken as he is taught in his new school. They all walked right past him, all these children who have known him for years and tolerated his eccentricities. The age has come where they see the difference. It confuses and annoys them, and frankly they have no time for it. It's not hard to imagine why. A little boy constantly staring at you and trying to stroke you is hardly likely to encourage a four-year-old to want to play. But watching the constant rejection is like being rejected yourself. It's worse. It's watching the thing you love most in the world being rejected. I hope you never have to experience that, although I suspect most people will, at one time or another.

By the time hubby got home, I was in a pretty bad way. Nearly a whole bottle of wine down, eyes red from crying, and I had forgotten to buy necessary stuff from the supermarket. Not just necessary stuff, if I'm honest, but bread, milk and sugar. Surely it's the mark of the world's worst wife and mother if you forget the basic staple foods of the home? But my head this week is nowhere. It's with my oldest son at school as he struggles to find his way.

I hear reports from school that another child threw sand all over his head, and he just sat there. Where was I to fight for him? How can I possibly protect him? He is such a gentle soul. I want to teach him to fight back, to show the world that he will not take their shit. But I don't want to change who he is. Maybe his peaceful heart is the very thing that will be his gift.

As I fed, bathed and dressed them tonight, I cried continuously. Softly and silently, so as not to alarm anyone. Alex, bless him, didn't notice a thing. 'I don't want chicken! I only eat beetroot!' Ah, so my emotional state clearly didn't impact too greatly on his own mood. Sam is too young to understand anything he can't touch or put in his mouth. Jack, however, is Jack. He stared at me most disconcertingly, before reaching up his hand and wiping away a tear. 'Mommy, is you sad?' It's hard to know how to answer that question from a five-year-old. Especially when he's the cause of my tears.

I'm not a good enough mother. I know that. I try to convince myself otherwise by sticking to certain things such as routine baths and dinners. I love my children often physically by way of cuddles and emotionally by way of sincere expressions of love. But it's not good enough and it never will be. Because I spend a certain amount of time in the day away from them, either working or following my own personal dreams. I berate myself often, and imagine that people, including my husband, make jabs at my character. The slights I imagine from those around me don't come from them at all; they come directly from within me, and are directed entirely at myself. It's so selfish to follow your own dreams and desires when your children are so young. But what if it's the only escape you have?

19 February 2013

It's raining now, hard. It's comforting in a way, as it echoes the conditions in my heart. Last night was very bad. This morning I tried my best to be strong. First, a brisk walk on the farm with a couple of friends. Then the planning meeting for Sam's garden. I'm so excited to get started, and even more excited to finish and have my quiet space where I can talk to him. But the longing is big and heavy today, and carrying the burden has exhausted me. I am weary deep into my bones. Just finished dinner and now it's time to bath the boys. Such a lovely job, really, but it feels like a mountain I still have to climb this evening. But climb it I must, hard as it is, and somehow that knowledge helps me.

Bath time done. I got in with them, and that's the best I've felt all day. I must keep in mind, keep reminding myself that they are not a daily chore but my very reason for living. Jack and Alex are playing in the playroom with cars. Jack's incessant grabbing will soon put paid to that, though. It's like a nervous tic or something, and it's driving poor Alex demented. I think the reason I feel so down today is that I allowed myself to glimpse too far into the future. A future of birthdays, Christmas dinners and a lifetime of no Sam. Alex and Sam were just learning to play nicely together – typical boys with normal social skills. So easy. So naturally, simply, frigging easy it could have been. But now we're back to two. Poor Alex has withdrawn into television. I know it's no good, but how can I take it away from him?

I have made an appointment for Monday with a child psychologist, and I am taking both boys. She specialises in grief counselling, but unless the dear old gal comes to live with me for a few months, I fail to see how it will solve my problems. She can only give me tips on how to deal with it. That's the easy bit, lady. It's implementing those measures, re-enacting them over and over and over that's the hard part. And ain't nobody gonna pay me by the hour for doing it.

I got my period this morning. Not surprisingly, today I feel like my insides are bleeding.

20:25 pm
I can hear Peter putting the kids in bed: laughter and giggles. It's so reassuring and I feel much lighter again. I did add some colour therapy oil to our bath and I'm starting to feel quite convinced of the benefits. This one was designed to help us connect to our 'I am', and maybe it has. Call me a crazy hippy if you like, but don't knock it till you've tried it. And certainly don't judge me until you've walked in the heavy boots I will now wear forever.

I wonder if I should get the boys a puppy? We've been talking about if for a while, and maybe this is the right time. Something to look after... they both miss the big brother role so much already. But is it the right thing? Best consult the psychologist on Monday. My own studies were now so many moons ago. Much may have changed. I may inadvertently fuck the kids up completely. Choices, roles, responsibilities, each so immense and powerful, the possible effects so far-reaching. No wonder parents today are so exhausted – we overthink everything. I was always a lucky girl. Good at school, attractive enough (but not so gorgeous that everyone else secretly hated me), with lots of friends. Well-off parents, nice cars, two very cool sisters and a brother. Lucky, lucky, lucky. And thus I skipped gaily through life. My parents' less-than-perfect marriage and various ups and downs floated over me and my siblings, largely because we always had each other. There are four of us and our bond is very strong. There is Sensible Sister, the oldest. She is brilliant, accomplished, organised and the glue that pretty much holds us all together. Then comes Arty Sister, wildly talented, gorgeous and impossible to pin down. Then there is me, the third girl, sometimes responsible, sometimes impossible, but just loves to have fun. Lastly comes The Brother, forever little brother to us all, although a grown man with a son of his own and a good head taller than any of us.

We had everything we needed, and blocked out anything unpleasant by cocooning ourselves into one bedroom and giggling all night. There were less-than-happy bits, for sure. My beloved sisters went off to boarding school first, and there were two long years until I could follow. I have little recollection of those years and little desire to dig too deeply. Perhaps not the happiest, but compared to the ordeals of many, fairly uneventful. My brother stayed on alone, and he carries his own scars, but that is a story for another day. Perhaps it was the sheer unexpectedness with which the rug was pulled out from under me that shocked me into sudden strength. Because Lord knows, I was about to need it.

I need very much to sleep now. I have taken a sleeping pill, but until now I have found these highly ineffectual. Let's hope I am proved wrong tonight.

1999

London was fun. I mean really, really fun. I met some of my best friends there, despite having to share horrendous sleeping conditions with them. And occasional boyfriends. Of course, we had what we considered to be problems: not enough money for decent wine, and could we scrounge together the entrance fee to the local club on Friday night? Once inside, we were skilled enough to ensure that drinks kept coming from starry-eyed boys without a snowball's chance in hell. After five years at university, London was just what I needed. The intention (as with many South Africans) was to earn enough pounds to pay off my student loan on my return. Alas, that was soon the furthest thing from my mind, and any spare cash was quickly distributed between Topshop, Boots and the Black Horse pub. Life was pretty damn good, it cannot be denied. There was the occasional tearful phone call home, followed by the immediate transfer of funds to ensure my survival. I guess somewhere in the back of my mind I was aware that my father's illness was progressing, but such banal issues remained a world away.

Then, in October, the great upheaval. Another tearful phone call, this time from my mother to me. There was no-one else for her to call, really. My oldest sister had recently married, my second sister had a young son to take care of, and my brother was much too young. 'Please come home,' was the message. 'I really need your help.' Not words I ever expected to hear from my strong and capable mother.

By the time I got home, it was clear things were far gone. My father was desperately ill with emphysema and had suffered a series of small strokes. It was the strangest thing to see this man hunched over, no longer walking with ease, but shuffling around the house like a strange, ghostly presence.

Dear old dad hasn't had much of a mention so far in this journal. Perhaps it's time I told you a bit more. Extreme intelligence is a blessing when used correctly on your life's path, but a curse when wasted and frustrated. It was only later, during my psychology studies, that I looked back at my childhood and recognised the signs of bipolar disorder in my own father. Coupled with his alcoholism (which was cause and which was effect is now impossible to examine), this made a man of severe contradictions. There is no doubt that he was brilliant with a razor sharp wit. But often this razor was used to cut people deeply. Never us children, or not intentionally, but my mother bore the brunt of his anger against himself and his thwarted dreams. He loved us fiercely, but the only way he was able to show us was through material gifts. And, although nice to receive, money isn't what children most need from their fathers.

He never lost his sense of humour though. He could hardly speak, but he did try to communicate with us through various grunts. My siblings and I would be sitting in the tiny, depressing lounge just off his bedroom, and he would try to talk to us. 'Croak, croak, croak,' my father would say, and we would take turns in a guessing game. 'What's that dad?' 'You need some wooden benches?' 'There's a war in the trenches?' Then we would laugh like drains, my father the loudest of all. Humour was the way we handled things in our clan, and to date it seems to have kept us all reasonably sane.

20 February 2013

Today was better. Not great, but then it's hard to imagine things being completely great ever again. But they will be one day, won't they, Sam? Tributes keep pouring in from people we know and people we don't. A friend wrote the most beautiful blog about your memorial service, with a message of hope, rather than just sadness. That's exactly what we wanted, isn't it my boy?

I didn't tell anyone to wear turquoise. It's unclear to me why I even decided this should be the colour of you. Yet on the day, so many guests turned up wearing shades of turquoise, and I wasn't the only one to notice the coincidence.

The night before your service, I found a turquoise pashmina in my cupboard. I'm not sure where it came from; I'm quite sure I never bought it. But it was perfect. I was wearing a black dress to the memorial but I knew you would love some colour. I showed my sisters in the lounge and they agreed it was just the thing. At 7:26 the next morning I got a message from my friend M, who was, I might add, not in contact with any of us. 'Have you got a blue scarf? Sam would like you to wear it this afternoon.'

And I believed just little bit more, and another tiny bit of healing took place.

Our home had filled up with people who love us, all desperately helping in whatever way they could. Hubby's family were amazing. His sisters came from the UK, his father and wife from Johannesburg, while his mom and her husband teamed up with my own family to cook, clean and take care of us. All of them put aside their own grieving to help us cope with ours.

Your service was awesome, and I had so little to do with it. My friends and family sorted everything out, and the village put together a working group for food preparation. It was big, with over five hundred people. I would love to write about it, but I think other people's words would be more appropriate here. Your life touched so many, my boy, and this is only the beginning of our journey together.

Fred Hatman wrote:

Four days later I stood on a beautiful farm just outside our village and, with you and you and you and you, paid tribute to a little life lost. There is little comparison to be made with what I had experienced a few days before except, once again, I was taken on a painful and extraordinary journey. It was so hard. And (I almost can't write this) it was indescribably beautiful. I don't really understand. I know I was rubbish at science at school but I no more understand how our planet spins on its axis than why life is taken away from some. But I know we are not expected to understand. We are expected to learn. And I learned a lot on our own Turquoise Friday at Stanford Hills Estate. I learned that, no matter how hard I might want to try, I could neither share nor lessen the pain felt by Pete and Jami. Or any parents who lose their child in any of the tragic circumstances that the universe has found to take them away. I learned that Sam had been a brave little guy with a beautiful personality. I learned that he was Super Sam. A superhero. I learned that he had been born with a full head of hair. And a heart of gold. I learned that life is more precious than I had come to believe. And more fragile than I ever dreamed possible. I learned that chimes hung in a tree can sound unimaginably eerie. I learned that plants brought by friends can make a beautiful garden. I learned that Dylan's

'Blowing in The Wind' can be almost unbearably evocative. That people can sing and dance and be strong and cry all at the same time. That people's eyes can tell us so much. That a hug can do the job when words fail me. And that the words spoken and sung and thought and felt and enclosed in huge droplets of tears about Sam and his family carried enormous power. The kind of power that switches on our hearts and makes us beautifully human. And I learned that, just when sorrow and pain threatens to become too much to bear, the release of a bunch of balloons into Stanford's kind and smiling skies can uplift us. And give us some sort of release of our own. Yes, I learned that I don't know very much. Or understand. And I learned that I know, no matter how trite it may sound a lot of the time, that love is truly all around. And that it is all that matters.

Nicci Cloete wrote:

Chanting 'Om' for Baby Sam I Am

Last Friday I had the incredible privilege of being a part of a memorial service for an eighteen-month superhero who left this world too soon. He was the son of a school friend, and although I was never fortunate enough to meet little Sam, by all accounts he was an absolute legend. Judging from the turnout at the memorial service and the way people reacted on the day, this little dude was something special indeed.

As a mother of a four-year-old and a two-year-old, this whole tragedy was painfully close to my heart, and I confess that I spend the entire weekend after I heard about the accident in floods of tears, and spent more time at my meditation bench, with a candle lit for my friend and her husband and two remaining sons, than I recall doing in recent times. I cried when I woke up, I cried when I went to sleep, and the only thing I could do to start to make sense of this senseless situation was to meditate and try to send love, light and acceptance to the bereaved family.

35

I wasn't the only one – as the news spread, friends kept contacting me, asking if it was true and whether I knew any further details. We were all grieving, not just for the family and the deadening loss of this vibrant child, but for every single parent that ever has to experience this despicable turn of the natural order – no sweet quotes can ever make up for a parent having to bury their child.

The memorial service was simultaneously the most moving, emotional, harrowing and uplifting experience I have had in my life. As I arrived, the late afternoon sunshine was twinkling diagonally across the field in front of the graceful old Cape Dutch house, the oak trees were dancing in the wind, and there was the sound of a piper on the breeze – anyone who has heard this before will know what a haunting and emotive sound this is. Upon seeing the beautiful shrine set up in front of the natural marquis, with framed pictures of the precious little Sam, the white candles, wind chimes and bouquets decorating the oak trees around the tent, it was immediately apparent that this was going to be something to be remembered. The parents had asked for people to bring a plant to remember Sam in a memorial garden, and the beautifully delineated garden was literally bursting at the seams with all the offerings. I love to think how that garden is going to thrive as the years go by.

The service started with the most beautiful song, 'Precious Child' by Karen Taylor Good, and it was at this point that I gave up trying to stem the flow of tears, and instead allowed them to stream down my face as everyone ached along with the incredibly brave parents. We were all united through our floods of tears and an astronomical respect for the family for how bravely they are handling this tragedy and what incredible support they are managing to provide to each other, even through their own personal pain.

The eulogy read by the mother – the beautiful, brave mother – brought everyone to their knees:

Our baby boy, our source of joy
Our brother and our friend,
We loved you then, we love you now
And this is not the end.
Your freckled nose, your cheeky grin,
Your big blue eyes shone from within,
Your joyous shouts of 'Gotta go!'
This world for you was just too slow.
The way you lived, the way you loved
Was so intense and pure,
And we hope that you felt treasured here,
Because, by God, you truly were.
An old soul is what we called you
And that is what you are.
We feel your love around us now
To help us heal these scars,
You may not be here on this earth
But in our hearts you are alive.
We are today, we'll ALWAYS be
A family of five.
Love you always, Mommy, Daddy, Jack and Alex

We cried, we wept, we admired everyone who made a beautiful speech, and we applauded the farm labourers who showed their love for the baby himself, as well as a deep love and sense of respect for the parents. When hundreds of balloons were released – white to symbolise all the spaces that will be left behind by this beautiful baby, and blue to symbolise all the tears we will all shed that will be sent up to heaven rather than falling to the ground – we all watched them rise high into the sky and then drift off with the wind over the Overberg and into the great unknown. This was possibly the most heartrendingly beautiful part of the whole ceremony.

I have nothing to offer to the mother and father of this precious child, gone too soon. I am not religious, but my sense of spirituality deepens with each passing year, and especially with each passing person. So many people have written such beautiful things, and I can't compete. So, simply, a few words:

When my precious granny passed away on 2 August 2012, I feel that I was fast-forwarded into the realm of pondering what's beyond the here and now. My granny, Patricia Brink Langley, was not only the most stylish babe one could ever meet but the most wise, humorous and calm person you can imagine. She practiced yoga from her early days in then-Rhodesia, and she is most definitely the reason that I fell in love with the practice myself. For months since she died, I have felt that every time I ended a class and led the class in chanting 'Om', it was all about Patrish – that's who I hold in my mind's eye, and I as I bow my head as the class ends, I see her face and almost hear her saying in her gentle voice, 'Hello darling.' But now, every single time I prepare to get up off my yoga mat, she shares that precious moment with Sam, who is also front of mind when I turn my attention to the beautiful universe and trust that all is happening as it should.

I can't imagine how you would ever make sense of the loss of this little/huge person. I see Sam everywhere. I keep you in my mind all the time, J and P, and that's all I can do.

Do you see, Sam, how big you are? Is it starting to make sense to you? Because I read these words and I feel the tiniest little sparkle of hope as your message reaches the world. Don't forget that I will love you my whole life, with my whole heart.

21 February 2013

I went for a long walk on the beach today. It was a weeping walk, but I felt you near me all the time. And I even had a butterfly go past me – on the beach! What are the odds of that? Butterflies are everywhere suddenly; I am surrounded by them. And each one I see feels like a hug from you. I can almost feel your podgy arms tight around my neck and your softer-than-possible cheek against mine. I would give anything and everything I own for one last cuddle from you.

After the beach walk, I had a really strange experience. I am still trying to process its meaning myself, but I do know deep in my heart that it is a message of love and forgiveness. I was driving away from the beach, slowly, as my eyes were still spilling over with tears. The car behind me was clearly getting annoyed, so I pulled off into a road leading left. And, in order to go around the block, I turned left again. And suddenly I stopped, because there on my right was a house I hadn't seen since I was five years old; a house firmly imprinted in my brain in the place where nightmares are stored.

House number 168. I got out of my car and approached the house, and the first thing I noticed were the butterflies. Not just one or two, but many. There was clearly no-one home, so I walked around and then climbed the outside stairs that led to the front door and also offered access to the large balcony.

I stood on the balcony, looking out. And I spoke to you, Sam. Why did you lead me here? A feeling of tremendous peace overcame me. A feeling of forgiveness surrounded me. I turned around, and was shocked by the proximity of the huge butterflies as I turned, each one the size of my head. They were decals stuck to the glass sliding door, but I hadn't noticed them as I ascended the stairs. My heart was beating so fast as I left, it felt like a butterfly was flapping its wings inside my chest.

22 February 2013

What is it you were sent to teach me, Sam? I think it's becoming clearer. And the clearer and more significant this tragedy becomes, the more I feel you around me, and with me, behind me and inside me. And God, that helps the pain so much.

I was playing cards with Alex and he was shouting, 'No Mommy, you must shuggle the cards first! Shuggle them!' He was obviously confused between shuffle and juggle. It was so cute. When last did I play cards with my boys before that Friday?

I realise now why you were always in such a hurry, Sam. Your first words were 'Gotta go,' and you repeated them hundreds of times a day. You never walked, you ran. Always picking up my handbag and heading for the car. How did I not recognise who you were imitating? Bloody A type, over-achieving me. Got to be chairman of this, leader of that. Always fucking running. And this is the cruel, cold, hard slap in the face it took to wake me up. So many people had told me, my baby had been trying to tell me, my body had been saying it, my inner self had been practically screaming at me *slow down, slow down!* But I didn't listen, or just got too busy to hear. I am so, so, so sorry Sam. I didn't give you enough, I see that now. And I won't make that same mistake again.

I really was doing the best I could, but I see now that my priorities were so screwed up. And I am desperately sorry that I lost you, that you are forever gone before I listened.

24 February 2013

Aimlessly trawling through my computer the other day, I opened a file called Diary 2012. Another of my haphazard attempts to create some order in my frantic life, to document it, to find the answers. The file has only a single entry, dated 8 February 2012. Exactly one year before the day that changed the course of our lives forever. And we don't believe in coincidence?

I can't sleep. I have so much work waiting for me tomorrow. And a lot more emotional stress. And I can't even get to fucking sleep. Maybe I should go and see Louisa. But where would I find the time? And what would I say? My life is just fucking hard right now. Nothing I can say to her is going to change that. Must not forget to deal with Robert Benier's order tomorrow. Must do the cash flow forecast. Mustn't forget Jack's got riding at 12. Mustn't forget to cancel my own lesson... simply haven't got time. Must remember to phone bank about Wilfred's funeral policy, but I already know they are going to say there isn't a valid one. Mustn't forget to phone Wilfred's grief-stricken family and tell them that. Must follow up outstanding payments. Don't forget to fill in green form for Jack's school. And fax Sam's birth certificate to the medical aid. Kids are behind with their immunisations. Should I just lose their clinic cards and pretend I don't know about it? Also, must go to dentist as have gaping holes on both sides of mouth, and can only chew on front teeth like a rabbit. Pick up donated flowers for funeral. Take Jack to Cape Town Friday to see new therapist. Must pay personal bills, and some company ones. Speaking of which, would be a good idea to actually recon my bank account and see where I stand. Ah well, what does it matter? Can't do anything about that right now anyway. Book accommodation for PK for party. Get quote for tent for party. Sort out Peter's 40th birthday present. Remember to arrange for transport from Johannesburg for the champagne glasses with luminous stems. Need to speak to Jack's speech therapist re exercises for home. Do budget plan for Stanford info event and hand to Councillor Solomon personally ASAP. Do I still have to pay that fucking Workmen's Compensation? Anyway, I'm sure you get the picture. Round and round and round it goes. There won't be much sleep tonight. And tomorrow will be exhausting.

Is everyone's life like this? Am I just being pathetic? I told Peter tonight that I'm not really coping. His response was that not coping is not an option right now. He needs me to cope, the farm needs me to cope, and my children need me to cope. And he's right. So what options are there really? I will google some inspirational quotes. I will buy multivitamins and energy boost tablets that I will forget to take. I will watch an episode of Survivor, have some tea and twenty cigarettes. And then I will get up tomorrow morning to three demanding kids and I will cope. Because there is no alternative. But wait, that can't be right. It simply can't be that I have to live in this state of constant anxiety and worry, despite giant yellow tablets daily, which are supposed to make me happy. So what to do. Re-examine values. Check life balance. Load of balls really. This farm still needs to run. The kids still need feeding and dressing and bathing and cuddling and fun time and therapy. But what do I need? At the moment it's not allowed to matter, but that can't go on for long. So here is my deal to myself. Today is 8 February. By the end of February we need to have a solid plan for our next move. And it needs to be one that looks better than the current plan, not worse. So that is what I will do tomorrow. I will stand up and

I will tackle shit, knowing that at the end of this month things will look better. I must put on my big-girl panties and deal with it. But there is an end in sight, for at end Feb I will assess the whole situation and we will know what changes need to be made. This is not a healthy life. It's unbalanced and it's making me unbalanced. So something will have to give.

See any clues there? Any signs that life was off course? You were my lesson, Sam. Not your death, that lesson would be too cruel. But your life is my lesson. I miss you, my boy. I want to hold you. I want you to come around a corner, catch sight of me and raise your arms and shout, 'Yay!' I want you to run to me and jump on me and hold me. But I can't think about that too much right now. The pain is still too raw. Instead I focus on my search for a meaning, and already there are so many. I did try to change my life for you, you see, and I almost succeeded. But decades-old personal needs and a pathetic burning desire to prove myself got in the way.

By March 2012, I was at my lowest ebb (before this one, that is). Simply too many balls in the air, and it's not humanly possible to maintain the necessary rhythm to keep from dropping them. I was fairly miserable, with no clear idea why, and certainly no clue as to how to go about fixing it.

No matter how strong you are, how smart, or how hard you work, this situation will break you eventually. You are only one person, and spreading yourself too thin to try and please everyone will ensure that you're never entirely fulfilled.

Yet sometimes, just when you need it most, someone enters your life, even if just for a brief moment, and changes everything. Through word of mouth ('coincidence') I heard about a woman recently moved to the area who had done wonders for the life of a friend of mine. She called herself a colour therapist, not a discipline with which I was yet familiar. This was indeed a surprise, as I considered myself something of an expert on alternative therapies.

Admittedly, most of it I had not taken particularly seriously. But I had always been the first in line for a reading: tarot cards, tea leaves, auras… I'd tried them all. Most readings were fairly vague and easy to apply to my own life in whatever fashion suited me, presumably by charlatans with varying degrees of skill in reading people at a glance.

So it was with some scepticism that I knocked on the door of a little cob house on a nearby farm. The house was more of a hut, with rounded windows and doors. Inside I made the acquaintance of a very mild-mannered Irish girl with whom I felt immediately at ease. And that moment was, in hindsight, the beginning of The Big Change within me.

I was directed to a table laid out with a strange array of chalky sticks in dozens of shades of colour. She left me alone for about ninety minutes while I did as instructed: simply drew on a large piece of paper all the important elements of my life, in whatever colour and shape appealed to me on whatever portion of the page felt right. My friends, family, job, dreams, fears – all were dutifully transferred to paper. And during this process I cried and cried. I sobbed as I drew numerous apparently meaningless circles, squares and triangles. I couldn't fathom where the endless tears were coming from. To me, this lingering feeling that I was unhappy was nothing short of ungrateful. For Christ's sake, any fool could see I was the luckiest bastard alive, with a husband who loves me, three healthy children and a roof over my head – a giant frigging roof on a beautiful old farmhouse, for that matter! What right did I have to be crying and moaning when people around me were hungry, lonely, homeless…

There's another LGT right there: everyone's problems are relative, but by God, everyone has them. The perfect life is a fallacy. Not so fucking lucky now, am I?

26 February 2013

I've been so busy these last few days, and in a way that busy has been good. I've had to focus on other things. Business and kids. This busyness has kept me strong, but I don't think it's altogether good. I'm so confused about how I should feel. I feel really bad (and I promise, Sam, I swear to you, I miss you like a physical pain sometimes, an actual, real squeezing sensation in my heart that scares me) about the fact that I am coping. Surely a good mother would live in sackcloth and cover herself with ashes? I would, you see. I want to. But it's simply not an option here. Your brothers need me to be strong. Your father needs me to be strong. But all the time my grief lies in the bottom of my stomach like a great lump of festering bile. I simply can't afford to access it too often.

But this afternoon I have. I got into my car and drove around the village. I pulled up at the river's edge, sat there and let myself dip into it. And I am so glad I'm alone, because even I don't like to hear the sort of wailing sounds that come unbidden from my throat.

28 February 2013

I am okay. I am strong. But what about my poor family, you may ask? Jack, God love him, is being an angel. Only concerned about me and his dad. 'Are you okay, Mommy?' he asks me all the time. And I say, 'Yes, Jack, I'm okay. I'm sad, but I'm okay.' Thank God my sisters were both here with me when he cracked and offered us a glimpse into his open wound. I don't think I could have handled that particular incident alone. Jack walked in from school, into our entrance hall and started to scream. And he didn't stop. He walked around screaming, '*No, no, no!*' but it was only when he started shouting, 'Don't touch me, get away from me!' that I realised what was happening. He walked from room to room, crying and wailing, 'My *baby*, my BABY! Somebody help me!' It was like watching myself. The sheer terror in his eyes was painful, as I tried to hold him and tell him it would be okay. Eventually the hysteria started to subside, as the four of us lay on my bed – my two sisters, Jack and I. His screaming turned to sobs, as he constantly repeated, 'My foot hurts, my foot hurts,' until eventually he fell into a deep and merciful sleep.

I guess I need to go back there.

It's a beautiful, sunny Friday afternoon in a perfect world. We have friends around. Five of us adults and seven children. The kids are all in the pool, our favourite place, and certainly Sam's. 'One, two, fee!' Sam keeps shouting, and launching himself off the step. He has just learnt to swim with armbands, and keeps bringing me his little red wings with cars on, saying, 'On, on, on!'

Then the kids finish swimming and go inside to watch a movie. I sit with my friends around the table, less than five metres from the pool. Maybe five minutes pass, maybe ten. I should go and check on Sam, I say. But I don't. At worst he could be throwing his chips all over the floor or grinding play dough into the lounge carpet.

'Well,' says my friend P, getting up, 'the pool gate is a bit open, so let me just check.'

'NO!' she shouts.

I can still see her stepping into the pool. I know that what she saw will stay with her forever, and I'm so glad I don't have that particular picture in my mind.

All hell broke loose, and at that point it felt like my mind clicked out. My husband and his good friend were already trying CPR when I approached the pool, and just once, for the very last time, I saw your naked little body, Sam. And I saw your blank eyes, and I knew. My mind went somewhere, I've no idea where. But my unoccupied body went berserk. I ran inside to phone for help, but when I got to the phone I couldn't remember a single number, not a single one. I remember Jack was there as I smashed the receiver down, over and over, breaking it into tiny pieces. My friend P tried to hold me, but my skin felt raw and painful, and I shoved her violently away. I just shouted and screamed for my mother, who miraculously appeared. How long that took I cannot tell, but suddenly she was there. And I remember the kindly doctor from next door and his wife as they corralled me into a corner like a mortally wounded animal. She held my head to stop me from banging it repeatedly against the wall, while he injected me with something. Something that burned, and the burning sensation was good, a relief from the absolute terror and pain, pain, pain in my head and my heart. And then I think I passed out.

Did he go inside to watch TV, and somehow slip by us all again? Did he somehow remain in the pool area as we focused on shuffling the rest of the kids inside? I really don't know, and it really makes no fucking difference anyway. It was no-one's fault, and it was my fault, and it was everyone's fault. Blame can never change what happened. To survive this, I have to believe that it happened as it did for a reason, with some greater plan, and could not have been prevented. I have to think like that, because the other way lies only madness.

3 March 2013

Ihad a really good, peaceful day today. And then, as I sat with my brother and husband on the stoep watching Alex ride his plastic motorbike, my peaceful world crashed. I remember you, Sam, trying so hard to ride that damn bike, and your little legs were just too short. Just a tiny bit too short. And so you never got to ride that motherfucking piece of shit. It's not fair, and I want to watch you ride that bike. *Fuck!* So I have snuck off to my room for some 'quiet time'. There's no such thing when my head is so full of thoughts of you. And it really, really hurts. I cry and cry and write. Just now I lay down, closed my eyes and asked (begged) you to let me feel you. Thank God I did. It's a slight warmness, like the sun shining, and a very light buzzing in my ears. And even if I'm imagining it, I don't ever want it to stop.

And what of young Alex? What a complicated, inquisitive and aware little soul he is. His overwhelming outward emotion has been anger. But is that because of the situation, or is it simply because he is three years old? He can go into a rage simply because I cut his toast wrong or didn't stir his tea well enough. Last Monday we went to see a grief counsellor/play therapist, and we have another appointment tomorrow. Frankly, I didn't think very much had happened. We chatted a bit, asked the boys about Sam and they completely blanked us. Then they got to play for forty-five minutes, each with a toy of his choice. (I am strong, I will get through this.) Not very surprisingly, Jack chose cars and blocks, and Alex chose guns, darts, boxing gloves and swords. I left the room while they played with the therapist, and then we went home. And that was it. We hadn't been in the car ten minutes when I heard a weird noise from the back seat. I turned around and poor Alex had tears running down his cheeks and his mouth was contorted into a strange shape. He was trying to tell me something. I pulled the car over and turned around in my seat. 'Mommy,' he squeaked through his tears. 'I'm really worried about baby Sam.' I parked the car on the side of the road and sobbed with him. Jack just kind of pretend-cried along, but I just knew that this was a vital and precious moment for Alex, a moment that could either help my boy to heal or screw him up completely. And so we cried while I told him about you, Sam, about the fact that you are not with us in person, but are all around us and know how much we love you. And above all, that you are safe and warm and happy. And, God knows, I believe that. I have to believe it or I would crack. And I can't.

We spent a good while crying on the side of the busy road while I answered his questions as best I could. Then he said he wanted to go and play Playstation, so we went home. Because life goes on. (I love you, Sam.)

I encountered a fresh new hell the other day when I attended a function where not everyone knew me. Because right now everyone knows me: they avoid me, hug me or stare at me, but they all know my story. But here I was, forced into small talk with strangers. I wasn't expecting the question, which was just plain stupid of me. But I was physically rattled when the very nice girl I was speaking to innocently asked a question I had glibly answered hundreds of times. Do you have children? 'Three boys,' I would always answer cheerfully, with a slight roll of my eyes. 'Keeps me pretty busy.' Those with children of their own would chuckle conspiratorially. But this time the question reached directly into my stomach and closed tight around my gut. In a split second I made a decision. 'Two boys,' I smiled. *Fucking Judas mother*, my head screamed, *you have THREE!*

I'm sorry, Sam. And you. Always three, but that doesn't make for an easy conversation.

I only just realised that I have, for the first time ever, a giant boil on my arse. Typical Jami style. As long as the exposed bits look okay the world will never know. I don't believe that everyone around me needs to see every gaping, weeping wound. The trouble is, those emotions must sometimes find a way out.

5 March 2013

Peter just came back from work and his eyes looked so desperately sad. 'Aside from the obvious,' I said, 'are you okay?' 'Just the obvious,' he said, and burst into great, heaving sobs. I can't help him. He doesn't want a pep talk. He wants Sam. So I sent him off for a bath and sob in some special oil. Sea blue; the colour of you, Sam. Some days are just harder than others. Some days I can't believe I'm surviving this.

But let me tell you more about my visit to the colour therapist last March.

For you, this person could come in the form of a coach, a minister or just a new friend. What you need is someone with wisdom who will listen to you and try to give you an objective opinion on your current situation. In my case, her name was Claire. She took one look at my tear-stained poster and shook her head. 'No wonder you're tired,' she said. 'You're completely burnt out.' Then the tears really started flowing. Finally someone could see beneath the cheerful, coping exterior to what I wasn't saying. That I didn't know what to do, and I didn't know how to change. Always running flat out. Running to what? From what?

The investigation into what I had drawn was fascinating. What did I learn? Some of it became clear that day, but most of it over the following months, as I took Claire's advice and did the things she suggested. None of it was easy, and some of it was horrible. But I knew that if I didn't try I might physically collapse. It's hard to put all the lessons I learnt into words, but I'll try.

The biggest thing that had brought me to this place was my job. At this point, hubby and I had been farming for six years. Farming is a wonderful lifestyle, but it's not for sissies. Often you're not in control, but rather at the mercy of the elements and unstable markets. But this I can do. The problem was my specific cog-place in this alarmingly complex farming wheel. The things I love – reading, writing, people, public speaking – none of these was present in my daily work. LGT: this will never lead to happiness or true success. My natural skills and God-given talents were withering and dying, and me with them.

My dissatisfaction in my work had leaked its poison into every area of my life. My creative side was being smothered, so I was searching for other outlets. Writing columns, heading up committees, leading protests into my perceived injustices in the world. Later, through therapy and exercise, I was able to see the reasons for this overly driven behaviour.

I was the third girl in the family with a father who desperately wanted a boy. I have spent my whole life testing myself against men in both my business and personal life. Even my name was a constant reminder of what I was supposed to be and wasn't: James Peter Yeats the fourth. But, ah feckit, another bloody girl. We'll call her Jami. The birth of my surprise brother eight years later, the *real* James, essentially wiped out my identity altogether. So I fought harder. For a while there it felt like I was winning. But critically, I hadn't factored in becoming a mother.

And this, dear gals, is where we have done ourselves a great disservice. Generations of strong-willed, powerful women have fought for our rights: our right to vote, to work, to expect equal payment and fair treatment. But at what cost? I suspect that the assumption was that once women were earning fifty percent of the family income, men would be forced to compensate by taking over fifty percent of the household and parenting responsibilities. And, bless them, many have been giving it their best shot. The problem is simply that they're not able to. The gist of the dilemma is this: they can never be Mother. We women have special gifts and extraordinary powers, and we must never forget that. But ours are not the same as men's.

I am in awe of the loving patience and sacrifices of the full-time mother, but I don't necessarily think the position is right for me. I need to work. But if man and woman work equally hard at things outside the home, who will ensure that the children get to the dentist, eat the right foods (mostly), have vitamins, get dewormed, and learn to share and be kind to others? At the same time, that person needs to ensure that there is toilet paper, shampoo, colouring-in pencils and three types of cereal. You can hire someone to do it, sure. No shame in that, and often a necessity. I have a nanny still who I love dearly, and I'd have three nannies if I could. But at the end of the day, the final responsibility for your children's welfare – social, emotional and physical – must be yours, because you are the mother. I learnt this lesson the hard way, through a woman we shall call E – but more about that later.

So, by this unquestionable logic, if men do fifty percent and women do fifty percent, and men (try as they may) are unable to take over more than twenty percent of the mothering, that's another eighty percent heaped onto you. Which is why us women are often not coping. And we need to find a way to fix it.

I really love my husband and he loves me, and in this we are truly blessed. But in the five years since we first became parents, how many precious hours and days were wasted on bickering? The fights were different, but all with a common thread. A constant competition over who did more, who was more stressed, whose turn it was to change a nappy, who needed a nap more on a Sunday afternoon, who had done more driving around of children, who had less time for themselves... With our lives the way they were, we were both winning this competition – and both losing.

My decision about my life at that time wasn't based on long-term needs or plans. It was because of Claire's words that day, words my entire body knew deep down to be true.

'If I was a medical doctor,' she said, 'I would admit you to hospital and insist on bed rest. You are making yourself very, very sick. But if you do as I tell you, you have a chance to heal. Otherwise you will break down.'

I finally saw the severity of the situation. What good would I be if I were unable to function in any of my positions: mother, daughter, chairman, wife, director, etc? That was where I was headed. So that day I made a conscious choice to change my life, regardless of what obstacles might stand in my way.

8 March 2013

I am very worried about your dad, Sam. He seems so thin and tired and broken. I don't know how to help him. Please, my little butterfly, will you do something? Send him a sign to comfort him and let him know.

I want to tell you more about the butterflies. It would seem that (a) it appears to be butterfly season now, leading up to Easter, and (b) the butterfly is well known in most religions as a symbol of resurrection and the afterlife. I never knew that. Until this enormously painful challenge I now face, I never had any reason to research it. In the days following your death, I don't remember much. But when I started to emerge from the black haze, I had a clear picture of the butterflies you would send.

I've mentioned the first one, but I didn't quite finish my story. It was a yellow butterfly. Since then, this same butterfly, just the one, has visited me every day here in the garden as I sit at the outside table and write. When The Brother arrived last week, it was outside at the car to greet him, his fiancée and their baby Jonah – especially to bless Jonah and let him know he is welcome. Of course, it's been a bit strange having a nine-month-old, starting-to-crawl, my-kids-are-besotted-with-him baby staying with us. Our memories are recent and sometimes overwhelming. But we have been working through it, our whole family gradually allowing ourselves to hold Jonah and love him. It's part of the healing. Only once did Jack ask me, 'Is Jonah going to be our baby?' And I gently told him no.

On that day of the butterfly, I went out to visit a friend for the first time, my best friend N, my true sister. For about six months before your death, our relationship had been severely strained. First, a fall out between our husbands affected our relationship, although we tried desperately to ignore it. Then a number of harsh words, petty squabbles and issues created a seemingly impenetrable barrier between us. But on that unbearable day I had lain on my bed and screamed and cried for her. And she came and never left. Another healing by my powerful boy. Sitting on her familiar old stoep, glass of wine in hand, she gave me a card from a mutual friend. And on it was a butterfly. So I told her the story of your butterfly, and we cried. And then, right next to us, appeared the same yellow butterfly. It just swept in and floated away. And I was so glad she had seen it.

On my way home with Jack in the car, as we drove through the village, Jack suddenly said, 'I want to go to P's house.' This was another relationship desperately strained, but for different reasons. Of course, you know she found you, Sam. Her own memories and grief must have been enough to deal with. But directly after your death, my oldest friends and immediate family closed ranks around me. While I lay broken and beaten, they put up No Visitors signs around the farm. They sent messages (oh my God, the butterfly is here flitting around me – I knew you would come!) to tell those who they felt had not earned a lifelong right to see me so nakedly grieving. And that made my relatively new but very dear friend P feel very cut off. And there was nothing I could do about it. But on that day I pulled up at her house.

Another familiar stoep, another glass of wine and more tears. And once again I spoke about the butterflies, and a yellow one (the same one?) appeared and flew past us. Even she was comforted and admitted she had never seen butterflies there before. So that was the start, that day, and I expect you will send me these signs my whole life long. I hope so.

I can't begin to tell you how relationships have healed and strengthened. Everyone close to me is closer, and those who drifted away are back. Well, those that matter, anyway. The same applies to my husband. While driving around the farm the other day, I nearly drove into a ditch from shock. There was my husband on his motorbike, and sitting on the back, holding tightly to his sides, was my friend N's husband. The two hadn't spoken for about a year. But on that terrible day he came over immediately. It's amazing how trivial such disagreements become when tragedy strikes. Friends all stepped up to help hubby with his work on the farm. I guess that's how men show love and support for each other. Poor them, really. They don't have the luxury of sobbing away while painting each other's nails and drinking tea. A most comforting ritual, that.

The most powerful thing I've yet seen you achieve, though, is one I never thought possible. My mother could not, simply could not, endure mention of my father without launching into a litany of his faults, mistakes and transgressions. The festering anger and bitterness she held inside often bubbled to the surface unexpectedly. I feared it would make her sick, and tried many times to talk to her, to tell her it was unhealthy. But at that stage I still harboured anger of my own.

About a year before you died, my mother and I went to see an angel reader. One thing she said stuck with us simply because it made no sense at all in our lives, and therefore seemed like utter bollocks. She told my mother, 'Your husband is sorry, and he's standing waiting in heaven holding a bunch of sweet peas in his hands. Does this mean anything to you?' My mother scoffed. 'Sweet peas? I know nothing of sweet peas. I've never grown one successfully in my life.' The angel reader, whose name 'coincidentally' was Sam, said simply, 'Maybe it will become clear later.'

It was a very different mother-daughter pair who sat outside a year later in February 2013. More open, and more broken. My friend C was sitting with us as we researched Sam's colours and birthstones to use in his memorial service. Then we came to the flower of his birth month. 'How lovely,' said C. 'It's the sweet pea.' It had been a long time since that reading, but something instantly clicked in both my mother and me. He had known, and he was waiting.

Three days later my mother cried and told me, 'I forgave your father last night for everything.' How very powerful is that, my butterfly boy?

October 1999

I arrived home from London to find the family's flower export business in a shambles. My dad had been a gambler, both literally and figuratively, but he had had great success at times, and somehow there had always been money. Now his illness has left him unable to work.

While my father lay wasting away in the room next door, my mother and I fought tooth and nail for that company. And damn, I'm proud of what we accomplished, and it will bind us together forever. I travelled, sponsored largely by the Department of Trade and Industry, to find new markets. Somehow we found sponsorship and grants, and I, the spoilt university girl, met strangers in foreign countries and fought to sell them products I knew nothing about. My mother, terrified of anything electronic, learnt enough about computers while I was away to do the invoicing on the South African side. Often we had very little idea of what we were doing, but by God, we became good at faking it. And we learnt fast. By 2001, sales had quadrupled.

But as my father lingered, with us yet not with us, things became increasingly difficult. To avoid another fall, he had to sleep in a hospital bed with high pull-up sides. A big white cage with bars around the sides, where he struggled for breath and soiled himself. There was no money to even consider moving him to a home at that point, so we just got on with things. We would work away in the home office, sometimes trying to ignore the insistent *clang, clang, clang* from the room next door. We tried our best for him, but anger and despair hardened us at times. It took me many years to forgive myself for that. The clanging was the sound of his wedding ring (oh, the irony!) that he would bang against the metal bars of his 'cage' to summon us. And, Jesus, it was a horrible sound. But not as bad as his rasping, laboured breathing. Sometimes his struggle became so unbearable that we would be forced to take him to the local hospital, which cost money we didn't have.

I remember my mom and me trying to carry him to the car. He weighed so little by then that we could carry him with ease, but the strength of his fingers surprised us as he clung to the bars, terrified and desperate.

It was a terrible time, but we got through it because we had to, as women often do. In October 2003, my father finally allowed himself to die. Maybe he had seen enough to know that we were strong and capable, and that we would be okay.

10 March 2013

Ijust walked into my sister's kitchen in Cape Town, and ate and ate and ate. Not because I was hungry. I ate toast and chocolate and grapes and yoghurt. Never have I tasted anything so delicious, all so sweet and smooth and crunchy. I realise now that I haven't tasted a single thing for more than a month.

I arrived here yesterday afternoon. It's the first time I have left my boys overnight since we lost you. They stayed with Grandma, which they loved, but the worrying for me was never far away. I came here, where both my sisters were waiting, to a place of safety. When I arrived, I was overcome by the most incredible fatigue I have ever felt. It felt as though, bit by bit, my body was shutting down. I could hardly speak. My sisters sent me off to bed, where I slept a deep and dreamless sleep.

I realise why I am so tired. Staying strong for my husband and my boys is heavy. It's like carrying a boulder on my shoulders, which saps my energy and strength every minute. But I cannot put it down, until I am away from them, and then the boulder rolls off me and onto the floor. Finally I am released to cry and crumble and feel.

This morning we had some tea and a walk in my sister's garden, a huge and magical space. Stretched between some ancient pines at the end of the property is a hammock on which I promptly lay down. My sisters knew (as sisters do) and wandered away together. Suddenly I was alone, and I realised that this was what I'd been missing this past week or two. Because alone in nature I am not alone at all. It is my blessed and very important one-on-one time with you, Sam. If I am totally silent in an outside space, that is my best time to connect with your greatness and your huge presence. It is an amazingly draining, loving, sad and beautiful thing. And then finally the tears come. They run and run, slowly but surely down the same little paths along my cheeks. I worry that they may carve permanent tracks into my skin.

Then I took a bath and lay and cried for what felt like ages, but also not long enough. I cried for myself, for you, and for our family. For all the magical things you were and could have become, and now will never be. And for who I was, which is now forever changed.

Then Jack and Alex arrived for lunch along with my mother, my brother and his wife and son, and I slept some more. Thank God for my family. I can never understand what crazy stupid fight could cause siblings to never speak to each other. LGT: if your relationship is good (and trust me, we do fight and get annoyed with each other), and if you are willing to forgive each other for trivial spats, your siblings will be the very best friends you will ever have. They will understand you and where you come from better than any friend you can make or any lover you may ever have. If it is possible, make your peace. Do not let material, trivial shit interfere with what could be your most caring and reliable support system in times of trouble.

A strange sort of day today. Usually my favourite times are with all my family together. Today all the cousins were together for the first time, as this is Jonah's first trip to South Africa. But one little physical body was missing, and everywhere I looked the blank space assaulted my senses.

I am strong, and I will get through this. In those quiet times, with the buzzing in my ears and the white warmth around me, I talk to you. And I am sure I hear you talking to me. 'Don't be sad, Mommy. Don't cry, Mommy. Don't be scared, Mommy.' I try my best to listen.

12 March 2013

In March last year the day I came home from my colour therapy reading, I quit my job.

'Ah, easy for you,' you're probably thinking, 'but not really an option for me.' Well, let me tell you, it wasn't really an option for me either. I had no other form of income, and my husband's salary alone could not support our (then) family of five.

(I love you very much, Sam. I just sat on the couch and pictured you running and throwing yourself onto the cushions, little legs in the air and your toothy grin. Every day I miss you, little one.)

I was at the time a director of a business with three partners, one of whom was my husband. We had entered into this deal and purchased the farm based on an agreement in which I was in charge of finances. And now I had to tell them I was out. I took a leave of absence from my various commitments, and learnt to say no.

I gave myself four months to heal, and after that I knew my path would be clearer. In those four months with no income, the lack of financial independence was very hard. But what do you do when the choice is between the status quo and your sanity? It was never going to be easy. I did not discuss this decision with my partners; I simply informed everyone that this was how it was going to be. When it comes to major decisions about your life and happiness and future, only you know what to do. And regardless of what is standing in your way, if you make brave and sensible decisions and follow your gut towards your true path, the universe will allow things to fall into place.

The first thing you need is silence, peace and time alone. Maybe at first it's just an hour in the bath at night or a walk on the beach during your lunch hour. But you must be on your own. All the answers you need are inside you. You just need to listen.

14 March 2013

Oh God, Sam, why does this have to be our path? Why does it have to be this hard? I miss you. And for some reason tonight the grief has broken through my skin again, and the tracks along my cheeks grow ever deeper. There is no escaping it, so instead I immerse myself in it. I grab a big handful of still-couldn't-open-them sympathy cards and tear open the envelopes. I sob as I read the beautiful messages of love and hope, on beautiful cards with birds and stars and angels. But I need one thing, and I am looking for it while telling myself I am not. Then, finally, on the very last card I open here on my tear-stained bed, there it is. A butterfly. I think now I may be able to sleep.

16 March 2013

LGT: it really makes a difference to your life if you try to find meaning in what happens to you. Many have made the point that your life is based not as much on what happens to you but on how your react to it. And it's true.

What have I done in the last few days? I have planned and successfully pulled off our first wedding at the venue that has been my little business dream for a while now. I had up to twenty people in and around my house for a week. I ran around shopping for wedding stuff like a woman possessed. It was truly, truly fun and I loved it. And today I am unable to walk at all. My ankle is sprained and swollen like an overstuffed sausage. Isn't that clever? Been going too fast and the universe sprains my ankle. Amazing. So now I must sit and spend time in my head with you, Sam. And write.

The wedding was that of my darling, much-loved little baby brother James (the name thief, ha ha!). But before I tell you about the wedding, let me finish telling you how I got to this place.

During my 'sabbatical', one of the first things I did was to take better care of my physical self. For example, I had been chewing rabbit fashion for months: cavities ignored had made chewing on either side of my mouth impossible, but I just never got around to seeing the dentist. At what point had looking after my own needs become so low on my list of priorities? So I went to a dentist, who lined up a series of appointments for the coming months, and bit by bit we tackled the problem. For me, fixing my teeth was a physical act to show love and respect for the body that (despite some serious abuse from my side) has always served me well.

Another example was my big toe. The nail had started to lift from the skin, and my sister had told me it was a fungal infection I had to sort out, so I'd bought some very expensive muti at the chemist. But six months later I had yet to apply it to my bloody toe! Deep down, it felt like I must really hate my body to punish it so. Instead of my three-minute morning shower, I started to take long baths at night, after which I would spend a good twenty minutes rubbing creams and oils into my skin, and showing love to my physical self. Watching my toenail heal was surprisingly cathartic. And I began to feel better.

These baths also served as me-time and precious alone time. Bath salts, a candle and a little chat with the universe changed the way I spent my days, and I had more focus and less noise in my head.

I also read self-help books, piles and piles of them. I devoured them and (this is key) did all the exercises. Some of them were bullshit, truly, but others made real sense to me in my search. *Finding Your True North Star* by Martha Beck was one, but every book I read contained at least some wisdom, which I kept while disregarding the rest. I wrote positive affirmations and stuck them where I would see them; I made a storyboard of my hopes and dreams; I drew and I painted. My husband rolled his eyes and sighed, but even he could see the positive change in me.

I saw a psychologist with whom I cried and poured out my heart about the grieving I had done over Jack. Make no mistake, if you have a child with special needs, you do need to go through a grieving process. The hopes and dreams you had for your child are not going to come true as you planned. You will dream new dreams and find fabulous joy, but just not in the way you pictured it.

I used pastels to draw the various chapters of my life, from the first memory I have. And this really clarified for me my beliefs and my reactions to certain things.

Most of all, I knew I must write, but I wasn't yet ready. I may not be in line for the Nobel Prize for Literature, but writing is what I do. The act of doing it brings me peace as only doing what you are meant to do can.

Since you left us, Sam, I cannot stop writing. The words just keep coming and I need to put them on paper. Another glorious gift from you, my son.

I took long walks. I walked to the sea where I spoke to my mother's people, and I walked to the mountains where I spoke to my father and his people, asking for help and guidance. Sometimes I felt a bit stupid doing it, but every day my insight into the complicated and vast strings holding our universe together strengthened.

By the time I realised what I should do with my life it seemed so obvious and so simple. I couldn't quite believe I'd never realised it before, but, of course, I had never taken the time to look for answers.

I knew I loved writing, but suddenly I felt very aware that this was more than just a hobby. It was my calling. But that wasn't enough, because it's very tough to make a living from writing alone.

My whole life I have loved throwing parties, as had my father. Nothing gives me greater joy than watching people have fun at an event of my creation. I love people, and my work in the office had been a soul-destroying, solitary affair. I needed to become an events planner. There were obstacles, of course. At this point, my finances were in a shambles. But once you discover your purpose, your 'thing', and commit to it, you can make it happen, with positive thought and concrete visions of your true dreams. Because that is how the universe is designed.

17 March 2013

The wedding was beautiful. That morning we found ants in the couscous; then the starter, a giant pot of roast tomato soup, fell over and a fair portion spilt onto the floor of my car. The horse unexpectedly bolted, causing one of the bridesmaids to fall off the wagon onto the gravel. But luckily none of this happened in view of the guests, who were unaware of the minor glitches. And none of it felt like work or a disaster – just a series of challenges to be overcome. Because I love doing this.

Sam, this path is very hard. Your brothers are both sleeping in the room next door, and I can hear their soft snoring. But I look up from my bed and your cot is gone. It is simply not there, and nor are you. I am strong, I will get through this.

You were so special, Sam. You were born with a tooth, you know. You always had this one snaggly, slightly yellow tooth, and I fucking loved it. The doctor initially thought it was a cyst on your gum, but I had felt it and I knew it was a tooth. Then she said a neonatal tooth was very rare and that it would fall out in a week or two. But it never did.

Google freak that I am, I went home and looked it up. Some legends and cultures say it's a curse. Those I naturally chose to ignore. Some say it means the child is born for great things. Now I see that both can be true.

18 March 2013

I went out tonight. Actual out, to a birthday party where there were loads of people. And I tried so hard to be myself, to comfort everyone. But the problem is that 'myself' is now no longer someone they – or even I – recognise. I will never be the same. There is a dent in me, a scar on me, a piece of me missing. And it can never be fixed.

But the fact that I have changed does not all need to be negative. This loss will break my heart forever, but I can still move forward. In many ways, I am a better and more aware person than I was six weeks ago.

Anyway, it's ten o'clock now and I am alone. Jack and Alex are sleeping, and Peter is out with colleagues. And suddenly I can hold it in no longer. I have to allow myself to say it, just once. My baby is dead, and it is my fault. I am his mother, and I was supposed to look after him. And he is gone. I am so sorry, Sam. It's not fair, and I am not going to be okay. But now I must go to bed, because tomorrow I will be okay. You are safe and happy and warm, and you are with me.

19 March 2013

L ast night's ramblings were because of too much wine. Alcohol, a fickle mistress at the best of times, is not my best friend at this stage. It brings out the self-pity, which is such a pointless emotion.

21 March 2013

Yesterday was forty days. It feels very significant. Someone told me that when you cross over, it takes forty days to settle into your new spiritual self. After that, in your new form, it's easier to connect with those in this world. Forty days seems to be a recurring theme in a few religions, so maybe the common thread means something. I hope so.

Our big yellow butterfly is still around. Yesterday, for the first time, he was joined by another one, just the same. Alex and I sat on the grass for ages and watched them swoop and glide around us. It was perfect. I wonder what the second one means? Hopefully you have found someone to guide you, comfort you and be by your side. Maybe, just maybe, it's my dad. That would be something, wouldn't it?

Harvest on the farm is nearly over, and my brother is going back to Germany on Saturday. Life will return to normal. The new normal, that is, the one we are still getting used to.

We are ready to start planning for our new house. The second phase of the master plan, designed to give us the life we want, that our family deserves. It is much smaller than our current home, and I mean *much* smaller. We are building on a couple of rooms, but it will still be tiny in comparison. That's one of the best things about it. I don't need a huge house, especially if it comes with hundreds of people in and out, a total lack of privacy and piles of crap everywhere. When we move, we will take only the things we love. I am tossing all the unnecessary junk in my life – gone with chipped cups, unused fondue sets and twelve different egg lifts. What an amazing chance for a fresh start. I have looked forward to this for so long, and now I have to do it without you.

Funny thing about my foot. It is now bandaged and braced, and the doctor says I have torn my ligaments. It struck me yesterday that, on the day you left us, this is what I told your brothers. 'It's okay, Mommy has hurt her foot.' So what do you know? Now Mommy really has hurt her foot. A physical manifestation of my pain, maybe?

My sister spoke to one of her friends, who said (perfectly logically) that foot injuries are very telling. Something about a desire to move forward, but also a reluctance. That makes perfect sense to me.

It's weird, moving from this home. My children have lived here since they were born, and it's been a real honour to live in this house with so much history. But I know it's the right move. I've known it for years. Yet another 'coincidence' confirms it for me. At the risk of sounding crazy, I will relay it to you.

For seven years we have lived on the farm in the old manor house, a magnificent, sprawling Cape Dutch house with thick walls and high ceilings. We have been happy here, but as the farm's activities have grown, our privacy has diminished. My home is now officially operation headquarters. All washing and ironing for the self-catering cottages is done here; all cooking for events and for our small restaurant is done in my kitchen. My doors are always open, and staff wander in and out at all hours. During The Great Change, I realised that this lack of separation – between home and farm, family and work – was making me very unhappy. From the dreams of what we would like in our lives, a business plan had formed. We used this plan to procure the necessary financial backing, and now finally it is time. Phase One is to create the venue, now nearly complete. Phase Two is to move our family into the manager's house, now empty, and turn the manor house into a guest house.

When I tell people about the planned move, I usually spot some sympathy in their eyes. 'Poor you,' they think, 'to move from such luxury. What a step down.' But inside I'm leaping and rubbing my hands in glee. I want to shake them by the shoulders. 'Don't you see? It's not about the big house!' A big house can't make you happy, an expensive car can't make you happy. It's creating the conditions that are right for you and give you peace that will fulfil you. My needs are simple. I need a white bathroom with a bath. I need a covered stoep with a comfy chair to sit on when it rains. I need my privacy and I need my family.

Outside of my home I have other needs. I need to work. I need my friends. I need time on my own. But in my home I need only peace.

Still, I might have been feeling a tiny bit weird about moving, if you hadn't arranged for a sign.

I had not been to the manager's house in years. But on 7 February I decided it would be nice to have a braai down there. I invited my mother, my mother-in-law and her husband, and two of my dearest friends. And, of course, your father and brothers were there. The house had no furniture in it and you ran around like crazy, you three. Especially you, Sam. You were in every corner of that house, every inch. And we bathed you there in that bath, and we dressed you all in your little pyjamas (three pairs), and then we went home.

Your last night here on earth we were there, in our new home, surrounded by people who love you, and you blessed it. When things become clear it is such a beautiful thing. Thank you, thank you, Sam-I-am.

24 March 2013

I let hubby sleep in late this morning, and then asked him to take the boys out for a bit. They have gone planting acorns on the farm, and the table outside is blissfully peaceful. I lit a beautiful candle this morning. A five-sided anemone, one point for each of our family of five. It was sent to me by a woman I've never met. She heard my story and she felt my pain. Mothers know.

We said a little prayer as we lit it, your brothers and I, and I know that you heard it. I know that in all likelihood I sound crazy at times. I am going through a deep spiritual change. I don't know what to call it, but I need to talk about it. My darling husband usually pulls slightly squiffy eyes and indicates that he thinks I'm mad. But last night, when the boys were asleep, I sat him down and I told him. I told him about the way I'm feeling, the coincidences in my life, my belief in something immensely powerful beyond our understanding, which grows stronger daily. And I asked him seriously, 'Do you think I'm crazy?' He looked at me very lovingly and honestly, and said, 'No sweetie. I don't think you're crazy.' So there.

An exciting week lies ahead. Real, actual work on your garden is starting. We have sprayed the grass on the area, given time for the roots to die, and tomorrow we start the real, actual digging. I cannot wait.

Tomorrow the architect is coming, so we can start on the plans to renovate and move into our new house. Such big, exciting leaps to take.

26 March 2013

I am ready.
SAM

On 20 July 2011, Samuel James Kastner is born with a full head of dark brown hair, the biggest blue eyes I've ever seen (even bigger than his brothers', and that's saying something) and one scraggly tooth. Our third boy and the last piece of our puzzle. I get my tubes tied directly after his birth, so sure am I that our family is complete. And it is. When we bring him home from the hospital, he is an angel from day one. He hardly cries, just kind of squeaks a bit.

Sam is an incredibly happy and loving boy. Short and muscular, with the most infectious giggle, he is fast as a bullet, and strong. He can climb right to the top of the jungle gym, and then loves to slide down the ramp on his tummy. He loves water, and especially the slide down into the pool. There are five-year-old boys too scared to go down that slide, but at eighteen months he shows no fear. He loves being naked, and it's pretty tough to catch the little dude after a bath.

When he wants to get out of his camp cot in the lounge after a nap, he rocks it until it falls over. Then he rolls out onto the floor and shouts, 'Yay!' Oh God, he's a beautiful boy. Just like an angel. Everyone says so.

I can never replace you, Sam, and I wouldn't want to try. No-one could be better than you.

29 March 2013

After the roughest two days yet, I have woken up with peace and joy in my heart. Thank you, Sam. Peter and I danced this morning to a couple of silly songs with the boys, which was great. (Bloody 'Gangnam Style'... I could murder that guy.) During one particular line in the song, 'Waka Waka' by Shakira, something just resonated in me. 'Pick yourself up, dust yourself off and back in the saddle.' So that's what I'm doing today. For me, for you, for us.

I have cried for two days solid since the night I wrote about you. I went out and saw the full moon, and remembered you pointing and shouting, 'Moon, moon, *moon!*' And the longing was too strong. It overwhelmed me. But I will not let it win.

It's Good Friday today. What exactly is that? My knowledge of religion is shocking. Time for Google.

Aah, interesting. Wikipedia gave me the full rundown. I guess almost everyone is searching for answers, but for me this search has become crucial. The belief in something bigger, something beautiful and immensely powerful, is my way through this.

I went to church last Sunday. Voluntarily, on my own, in my butterfly skirt with my big swollen foot. Did I feel you there? I'm not sure, but I felt something. I haven't been to church in more than twenty years, other than for weddings and funerals. I really liked the singing and the praying bits, but the sermon just confused me. I shall have to investigate further. Clearly part of our journey, yours and mine, is to figure this out. And believe.

Another function at the Tasting Room today. A farewell snacks and drinks party for thirty people. Tomorrow we have twenty-four children booked for our Easter egg hunt in the vineyards, and a picnic afterwards. So it's working. Thank God.

Hubby needs to help me, though. The money section of my brain seems to be broken. I really don't care for the stuff, and would give everything away for free given half a chance. But he is a good businessman.

I met hubby in 2001, at the pub and restaurant he owned in Hermanus. It was called the Zebra Crossing and was a totally rocking little spot. We met there a few times, had coffee, had drinks, and went to see a crappy movie. One night we had too much to drink and some dancing ensued. He claims I asked him to come home with me that night, although that's not how I remember it. But he came and never left.

LGT: when you meet the right person, you will just know. There was an immediate comfort between us and we couldn't get enough of each other. It was like being in a private little bubble, as twee and soppy as that sounds. In my previous long-term relationship, I was jealous and it was horrible. I thought it was part of my personality, and it sucked. It's a horrible feeling. Of course, it didn't help that he cheated on me once (that I know of). I tried to forgive it, but something was lost. He was and still is a nice dude. But we didn't fit together.

Hubby has never given me cause to be jealous, and oh, what a wonderfully free feeling that is. I can come and go as I please and so can he, and neither of us has to worry that the other is cheating. Nothing is bulletproof, of course, but being able to trust despite not having any guarantee is the trick. Because we fit together and both of us know how lucky we are.

When we met, he was so different from me that we seemed an unlikely match to many. Especially my family. Me, spoilt university girl; him, party animal with skinny jeans (long before they were cool), earrings, tongue stud, and bottle blonde hair that was sometimes fire-engine red or in a Mohican. But there was an undeniable connection between us. Something just clicked on a very deep level. He brought out the rebel in me; I brought out his sensible side.

Nowadays, of course, we are both approaching middle age. We still have our rebel side, but now with two (three) children we have to keep it in check. Gone are the earrings and crazy hair, replaced by short back and sides, and sensible farm boots. But the real essence of Peter hasn't changed, not one little bit.

We did get tattoos a few days ago, after my brother's wedding. My brother got the words I AM tattooed on his forearm with a butterfly above them. Peter got a butterfly on his back. And me? Any surprise that it's a butterfly? A big blue one on my right foot. Much larger than I originally planned, but I love it.

You are with me, Sam. With every step I take.

29 March 2013

Tears again. But almost happy tears. They are tears of gratitude to you, Sam. For loving me, and us. And being with us. I am so sad that you had to go, but your leaving has taught us all so much. Know that we love you.

Last night was the first time Jack has said your name since you left. We lit a candle and sent you a message. He got really excited and said, 'I'm can send Sam a message?' I said yes. And he kissed your photo about twenty times and said, 'I'm love you, baby Sam.' Then along came Alex and demanded I light another candle for you. We're running low on candles, so it was just a tea light. And he gave his message. He is three years old and he said, very seriously, 'Thank you for living with us, baby Sam.'

30 March 2013

I was bathing the kids, and I casually mentioned Sam in a happy memory, as my psychologist suggested. I said, 'Remember when baby Sam was in such a hurry to get in the bath that he climbed in with all his clothes on? How silly was that?' Alex laughed and said, 'Silly Sam.' Then he asked why he can't see you anymore and if heaven is far away. Jack's eyes were wide with shock at the mention and asked randomly, 'Mommy, are you going to buy new chickens?' (Ours have done a runner, and no doubt been devoured by some kind of wildcat. That would have cracked me up a few years ago, but being on a farm you get used to it.) Alex was still busy babbling about heaven. And then he suddenly stopped and said, 'I want to call my chicken Mr Pete.'

Mr Pete was the name of my husband's favourite uncle's restaurant in Zambia. Hubby spent a lot of time there, and he loved his uncle dearly. So did I, actually. He was a right old lush, but clever and hilarious, and completely beyond control. He was killed in a car accident two years ago. He was so much the character behind his restaurant that he was naturally known to everyone as Mr Pete. How strange that Alex should be talking about heaven and then say the words Mr Pete. He never met him and has probably never even heard his name. Is he with you, Sam? Is it really possible to get messages from the other side? Or am I just going stark raving mad?

I sometimes feel a bit freaked out by it. But I know I have to trust this process, wherever it takes me. Because this is your gift to me, Sam.

8 pm
Fucking hell. Just when I think my heart can't break any more, something catches me by surprise. I put Jack and Alex in bed, said a little prayer and came to the lounge. Then Jack started freaking out, and I mean *really* freaking out.

I went to lie with him. In between sobs, in a strangled voice, he was saying, 'I very sick. It's too hard. I can't walk. I can't do nothing.' The saddest words I have ever heard.

It's because of the bicycles today. We decided to try them again, and today Alex just totally got the hang of it, riding up and down the porch. But Jack simply cannot pedal. And he's at an age where he fucking knows it.

1 April 2013

What a hectic weekend. Today is Easter Monday, and it's also 1 April – the date my husband first opened his restaurant, and also the date we took occupation of this farm. I know there is meaning behind Easter falling on the same date this year. Resurrection? New life, transformation, rebirth?

At the table where I sit and write, a stone has suddenly appeared. Well, not exactly appeared. I saw Jack put it here last night. He carried it from the house, from the table where we have your photo guarded by various angels and candles. But it's only now as I sit down to write that I see what has been written on it in black felt tip. I wonder who made it. 'Sam,' it says. 'The Lord your God is with you, He will take great delight in you, He will quiet you with His love, He will rejoice over you with singing. Rest in God.'

How very nice, and the culmination of all this has left me warm and fuzzy inside. That and the fact that after a heavy, but fun, weekend of parenting, the nanny is here! I have a cup of tea outside. It's been raining, and now the sun is coming out and the birds are all chirping furiously. It's in the small things, you know. LGT: be grateful for the small stuff; these moments will lead you to be grateful for it all, and this will make you happier. Tis God's honest truth, as my friend M told me: if you have a bath, really *have* that bath. Nice cup of coffee in the morning? Sit down and *enjoy* it. Be present and grateful for these small gifts and the rest will fall into place.

Of course, being 1 April also means it's April Fool's Day. And me, I love a good trick. If I do say so myself, 2004 was a particularly fine year, though I might just have taken it a bit far that time. We were newly married, and my dear husband was having all manner of trouble because of late-night noise and rowdiness at his pub. Great for business, but not for the neighbours, apparently. The police had been called a few times, and issued stern warnings while trying to stop the hordes from dancing on the tables. Most nights we were among them, back in the day.

With 1 April looming, I printed out official-looking notices of closure. I arranged with one of the barmen to sneak in very early and post them on all the windows. I'd also purchased a big lock and chain, which he wrapped around the door handles.

At 7:30 am sharp the phone rang. It was the restaurant manager in a mad panic, shrieking about being closed down. The staff were all sitting outside on the pavement in a state of shock. Peter leapt out of bed, pulled his jeans on, and rushed out of the door. I had to catch up with him and try to explain. He was so hyped up it took him ages to understand that it was a joke. It was very, very funny in a sick and twisted way. And eventually everyone saw the funny side. I think.

Today's trick was a bit more subtle. I know he loves me, but I do suspect that my husband thinks I'm bordering on crazy. And he may well be right. I think sometimes he worries that I may turn a corner and become a proper lunatic. So today I tried to illustrate for him the difference between mildly eccentric and proper bat-shit crazy. When he woke up this morning and made his way to the bathroom, he found me in bed, reading *The Journey of the Soul*, wearing a very fetching stainless steel bowl on my head, complete with a big, black and yellow butterfly on top. He looked at me quizzically. But as soon as I started to explain that the metal acts as a conductor, which makes it easier to receive messages from the other side, he burst out laughing. Slightly nervous laughter, I think, until I could no longer keep a straight face. Anyway, it gave both of us a much-needed chuckle. Mission accomplished.

I love you, Sam.

2 April 2013

Yesterday was pretty special. Just before sundown we were bathing the kids when a huge storm pulled in. Doors slammed and windows rattled as huge black clouds came rolling over the mountains. Just for a moment the rain stopped and a glimpse of the setting sun created a strange orange light outside. We all went out in our pyjamas (Alex still wrapped in only a towel) and I saw the most spectacular double rainbow I've seen in all my thirty-eight years on this earth. It was awe inspiring.

This morning it is still dark and raining hard. Only Jack and I are awake, watching Nemo for possibly the hundredth time. We tried the bicycles again yesterday. Alex sped away like a natural, while I pushed Jack. Interestingly, Jack told me he can't pedal, because he has a sore toe. Surely it shows some important development in his brain that he is able to make excuses for his own perceived and real shortcomings. Isn't that what we all do?

JACK

Boy One is special, and he's different. It's hard to define, exactly. From early on it was clear to me that his delays and low muscle tone had less to do with his body than his brain.

If I tell him something he usually gets it, but it takes a while for it to sink in. It's as if the messages bounce around in his head before they find their target. The same, therefore, applies to his physical movements. If I tell my leg to move, it does so without too much thought or effort. And if the height or gradient of the surface I walk on changes, my brain automatically corrects my body so I can take it in my stride.

Not so for Jack. Every step and action must be carefully planned. When the message is sent inwardly to his brain, it then hops around a bit before finally communicating that action to the right part of his body, or letting his mouth formulate what he's thinking. Likewise, his social interactions don't come naturally. Every reaction has to be taught to him, as his first natural action is to barge in and grab.

This is by no means a medical description, but I have lived with him and loved him for nearly six years, and so I believe I am qualified to formulate an opinion. We still have no diagnosis, and like an ever-increasing number of parents, I don't think we ever will. I guess the closest 'diagnosis' would be GDD-NOS, or Global Developmental Delay Not Otherwise Specified. Very similar to WHNFI or We Have No Fucking Idea. There is no guidebook, so we just have to bumble along and figure it out for ourselves.

At first I took the routes advised by doctors: physiotherapy, occupational therapy, speech therapy and every other kind of physical therapy. But what about his brain? What about helping that organ to function better? Not one doctor or therapist seemed to address that angle, which to this day I still find odd.

On 8 April 2011 I started a conversation with a woman on Facebook. She had been a few years ahead of me at school, and when my sister recently ran into her, she mentioned that she worked with special needs children. 'Ah well,' I thought, still on my continuous search, 'in for a penny, in for a pound. We may as well give it a try.' Finally I met someone who understood Jack's condition exactly, and I knew she was the one who would help Jack escape the shackles of his unresponsive body.

I am very fortunate that Y, the new therapist, does what she does for love and not money. Sure, it costs us, but we made special deals with her, and she was willing to negotiate. We embarked on a new programme during May 2011, just before Jack's fourth birthday.

The first step was a family workshop, where she explained the principles of Applied Behavioural Analysis (ABA) and how it can be applied to retrain and strengthen neural pathways. It's a one-on-one method of tutoring that works largely on constant repetition. This forces neural pathways to develop. With each repetition, the myelin sheath thickens around that particular newly created synapse.

Or pretty much like that. I ain't no doctor. The important thing is that it works. I've seen it. I'm not saying it's a miracle cure for anything or that it would necessarily work for other kids. I just really think it's worth looking into if you feel it could help your child. There is plenty of information on the Internet and tutoring videos to watch. And with so many children these days having difficulties (is it one in fifty-five children now on the Autism Spectrum?) it's worth seeing if we can get in there and bring them out.

After a good session of tutoring, my boy is more alert, his speech is better and easier, and his conversations more lucid. I know, because I'm his mother.

Y did an assessment, set up a syllabus, we trained a tutor, and we were off. It's a fairly intensive method with two hours tutoring per day. Initially it was hard, and it's painful to have to work through the resistance. But now Boy One loves and looks forward to his 'learning' sessions. It seems like a lot of extra work for such a young boy. It's a choice we had to make alone. With this level of therapy, there's little time or money for the more traditional routes suggested by doctors.

There will always be different advice from all angles. But as a parent you have to trust your instincts about what is right for your child. Because you know best.

18 April 2013

My trusty chef and assistant is on holiday, so I'm running the Tasting Room for the weekend. Today is Thursday so it's not too busy. It's lovely.

I'm sitting outside looking out over the dam and the valley. To my left is what will become Sam's garden. At first I envisioned a smallish garden, but the project has taken on a life of its own. The garden area is enormous, set between the vineyards and the olive trees just above the Tasting Room. It's on a slope, so hubby has been supervising the building of eight retaining walls built from natural rock in the area. This has all been hand chopped to create usable-sized rocks with which to build. There will be ten different levels in all, each with a different feel and theme, with steps leading from one to the next. And at the very top, under a shady tree, will be a butterfly bench and resting spot. We want the garden to be open to the public, and used by anyone who can benefit from its peaceful setting and message of hope. In this way we will ensure, my boy, that your name continues to be spoken and that you are never forgotten.

The garden layout kind of reminds me of my own spiritual journey. I learn something, I feel something, and then life gets in the way and I hit a plateau of sorts. It's pretty frustrating to feel so close to a big connection, a great discovery, and then feel it slipping away, only to be replaced by worldly worries about schooling, bills and chores.

Yesterday I visited Platbos, the ancient forest not far from here. It was raining as I walked among the gnarled old trees, but the drops couldn't reach me through the thick canopy. I walked and cried, and I spoke to you. I spoke about everything, about how fearful I am now that I fully grasp how fragile life is, and I asked for your help. As long as I strive to retain that feeling, that powerful connectedness (to you, to nature, to God?) I can sense you out there somewhere, and it feels like everything is going to be okay.

1 May 2013

As blessed as I feel, and as grateful as I am for everything I have, I will love and miss you my whole life with my whole heart. Crying again tonight, and frankly, I'm over it. I can't spend my whole life sad... what a waste of a life, Sam, both yours and mine.

What a sad, happy, up-and-down couple of weeks I've had. The boys are doing so well, and yet there are so many sad moments and challenges. Jack is still struggling to express his grief, and constantly worried about everyone, especially me. Just now my eyes were leaking, because I saw an unexpected picture of you. Jack came up, held my face in both his hands and said, 'Is you isn't sad, Mommy?' And his eyes were so full of confusion and despair as he wiped my tears away. Every therapist has told me it is healthy to show my grief in front of my children, but how can I when I see the pain reflected in their eyes?

Alex has changed so much in the past months. He is not so angry. He is incredibly loving. Our whole family has pulled together. Every day is filled with cuddles, kisses and 'I love you's. We have all seen how precious and fragile life is, and how things can change in an instant.

It's true for all of us, and the only way to make sure we get the best out of it is to live every single moment of every glorious day.

25 May 2013

Where do I even begin? Nearly a month since I last wrote. Why, I wonder? Why is it that sometimes the words just flow, and other times I look at my journal and I feel fear. I guess it's a lingering fear of not being good enough, of my words drying up or not coming out right. But I need to remember why I'm writing. These words only need to be right for me. And for Sam.

Sam. Always here. The longing never far away. Yet every day I grow stronger. I sit here today, a Saturday, at the Tasting Room. Lots of people are booked for lunch. Your garden is planted and I have a view of it to my left. It's beautiful. I can honestly say that I am stronger and more at peace than I have ever been in my life.

We planted your garden on a Wednesday, Sam. It took so long to prepare the soil, move the rocks and build the retaining walls that I was getting super frustrated. I woke up on Monday the 13th and suddenly knew the time had come. I sent out a message via Facebook to say we would be planting on Wednesday the 15th. Hubby put all his efforts and staff into ensuring we were ready. Suddenly the day arrived, together with so many friends carrying spades and gloves – even friends I hadn't seen for years.

Your brothers stayed home from school to help, with their hats and their spades, and we all dug and planted. It felt wonderful.

People are amazing, they really are. Everyone has their faults, but when the chips are down, I have seen that everyone is basically a good person.

Only when C points it out do I realise that planting day is exactly three months after your memorial date.

20 July 2013

Happy birthday, Sam. Oh God, I wish you were here.

Sam, the farm boy and his favourite toy

Me, seven months pregnant with Sam, with our old farmhouse in the background

Sam at the beach, his favourite place

*Sam, happy even in hospital
with a bronchial infection*

*Learning to eat on his own,
with limited success but much
enjoyment*

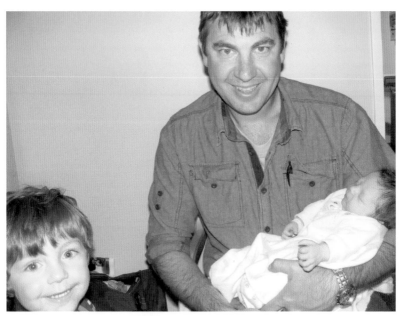

Alex at the hospital, delighted to meet his little brother

The brothers, December 2012

Our family of five

Jack taking care of his little brother

Sam and his Mommy

Sam being silly

Sam during the building of the Tasting Room

Me, hubby and my darling friend T at Sam's memorial

Releasing the balloons at the memorial

Trucks delivering compost donated by neighbouring farmers

Friends and family laying out the plants for the garden

Jack and Grandma Cathryn planting in Sam's garden

Joyful colours in Sam's garden

A special butterfly in Sam's garden, with the restaurant visible in the background

Alex planting in Sam's garden with his friend Joakim

Platbos forest and the Hard Pear tree, August 2013

Birthday card made for Sam's second birthday

Family wedding Left to right: Louis du Preez holding Johan, Jackie Yeats-du Preez, Lesley Yeats-Penn, James Yeats (with Jack Kastner), Maggie Tauscher, Peter Kastner, Jami Yeats-Kastner, Jamie Penn, Richard Penn

Carol Yeats, Jackie Yeats-du Preez, Lesley Yeats-Penn, Jami Yeats-Kastner, James Yeats

Crazy Butterfly Lady

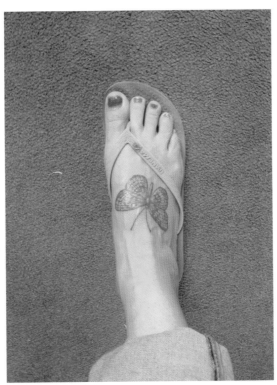

My butterfly tattoo

The Tasting Room restaurant viewed from across the dam

The old farmhouse at Stanford Hills.

23 July 2013

This morning I am sitting at my friend S's house writing. I only met her recently, but there was an instant recognition that we belong to the same tribe. She is someone who is searching, and has already started to discover. I'm drinking a surprisingly yummy, green tea and ginger concoction. The rain is pouring down, the words are coming, and it just feels so right.

I wasn't raised in an alternative environment. Well into adulthood, I was the first to guffaw secretly when there was any carrying on about angels and crystals and the like. That makes what I'm going through hard sometimes, the discovering and the knowing. But even more difficult is putting it down on paper where it can be judged.

Today when I leave here I am going back to C. Today we are doing a past life retrieval.

There, I've said it. So bring on the men in white coats. Somewhere in my head this has been the boundary of socially acceptable normality. But damn it, I cannot deny what I know to be true.

1:30 pm
I am sitting on a cliff by the sea after a fantastic morning of sobbing, laughing, writing, and consuming varied and numerous hot beverages. I have one hour left before my past life session and I want to spend it here, next to the boundless and infinite energy of the sea.

The sea is wild today, wilder than I think I have ever seen it. The waves are crashing on the rocks, showing their immense power with a dull thud and a spray of seawater high into the air. Every time the spray shoots up, *every single time*, I see a clear rainbow in the droplets. I asked for a sign, and in the past thirty minutes I have seen about fifty. How blind or blinkered must one be to ignore that?

You're doing the right thing, Mommy, you're on the right track.

If I believe that my boy is sending me messages (and I really do) then how much of a stretch is it to believe that we have lived before and will live again – that we live eternally? That we have contracts to fulfil on this earth, human lessons to learn, and hard as it is, that it's all as it should be? Not much of a stretch at all.

I have met enough people on this path now and spoken to enough enlightened souls about their own journeys to know that there are many of us out there. For every person who judges me as bat-shit crazy, there's at least one with whom the truth resonates. And maybe one day my words will help them to speak their own truth.

I can't wait to see what this new experience brings.

8 August 2013

Six months. One hundred and eighty-one mornings waking up without you in bed, curled up into a little ball with your bum in the air. One hundred and eighty-one days since I heard you say 'Mommy'. Since I heard you giggle. Since I saw your little legs pump as you run to the car to greet your brothers from school. And today I am allowed to dip into my grief. But I mustn't linger too long, or I may become trapped in this place of heartache. Neither of us wants that.

But let me light a candle for you, and let me say a prayer. So that you know when I dance or smile or laugh with my friends, it's not because I've forgotten you, but because I love you, I honour you, and I'm grateful to you every day of my life.

God, but your brothers miss you. There are many times when they cry for you, and say to me, 'I wish baby Sam could come back.' What can I do but hold them, and say, 'So do I, sweetie, so do I.'

Today I have been dancing. I have been rehearsing for the local village Broadway Extravaganza. It's so completely out of my two-left-feet comfort zone, but it was an absolute blast, and I'm really looking forward to the next rehearsal. Because life is short, my dear Sam, and dance we must.

9 August 2013

It was hard, yesterday, the six months. Harder than I thought it would be. But I spent a bit of evening time in Sam's garden, which is *so* my happy place. And the clouds were black with golden yellow rays streaking through them, lighting up the sky. Sometimes, Sam, if I really focus, I swear I can see you in everything.

13 August 2013

I love Tuesdays. They are my one true proper day off in the week. I drop the kids off at school, get a takeaway coffee, put on some nice music, and I drive. There is something so special about driving, about being between one place and the next where no-one can find you. It's one of the few times in my day that I'm really alone.

I turn my phone off on Tuesdays, which drives my husband crazy. But I have to do it. My time alone now is my time with you, Sam, and I'm not willing to compromise that.

Then I hide away somewhere, and I cry and I write. And it always seems to rain on Tuesdays here, which is perfect too.

Life is not a race. Life is not a race. This little mantra was recommended to me by one of my therapists. I have to remind myself all the time. Things move so fast, you have to shut it all off sometimes and take time out. How can you hear what your inner voice is trying to tell you when there's too much noise to listen?

15 August 2013

Just back from a day of deliveries and meetings with hubby in the big city. It rained a solid dark grey wall of water on the drive there. On our way back, we stopped at a high viewing point on the side of a mountain pass, looking out over valley and sea. The giant black clouds parted just enough to show great white streaks of light, which lit up portions of the ocean below like huge shining, silver discs. 'All this, just for us, Sam?' I thought to myself. 'How powerful *are* you?'

16 August 2013

Yesterday, on our way to an important meeting, it was raining hard. I was looking out for signs. Just as we arrived, a car in front of us had a random butterfly bumper sticker. Just before our destination there was a big billboard with a butterfly on it. I pointed these out to hubby, and explained that obviously a real live butterfly is the strongest sign, but sometimes you're unable to send them due to weather. He just nodded sagely and said, 'That makes sense.' Bless him. I wonder if he still thinks I'm a total nutter.

17 August 2013

I was asked to speak about you yesterday on a local radio station, Sam, and it felt strange but good. This really is such a personal journey, is it okay to share it? And then I got another message from someone somewhere in the world who needed to read this. And I know we're doing the right thing, you and I. Damn, it feels so good to talk about you, and to say your name aloud without crying.

20 August 2013

So much has happened these last weeks. I need to put it all down on paper, which will hopefully allow me to figure it all out. I have felt a tremendous shift inside myself.

The past life retrieval was amazing, but I'm sure I'll come back to that later. The gist of it is that it helped me to release the stuck feeling I've been experiencing, that lingering fear of finding my voice and speaking my truth.

Seemingly randomly, I started a blog on 7 August. Looking back now, I realise this blog has been anything but random. It's been coming for a while, and it's integral to my healing. I've received the most amazing messages from all over the world from people who have read it and been moved. And God, that feels so good to hear. It helps to know that I'm doing the right thing, because putting it all out there is sometimes one of the hardest things I have ever done.

21 August 2013

It's not easy to slow down. It takes practice. Quite often I forget and I find myself ragged, confused and irritable. Then I have to ask myself, when last was I alone? When last did I listen to the silence and let my heart speak?

23 August 2013

Someone very special to me lost someone very special to them this morning. They told me about the message you sent, Sam, to let them know that this is not the end. I know this will bring some measure of comfort. Your power continues to amaze me, my boy.

A dear friend brought me a book yesterday. It feels like it was written just for me. It's called *Hope for the Flowers,* and it was written by Trina Paulus in 1972. The story is my story, and most likely many of yours. It seems that forty years ago, old Trina knew something I am still busy learning.

> 'How does one become a butterfly?' she asked pensively.
> 'You must want to fly so much that you are willing to give up being a caterpillar.'
> 'You mean to <u>die</u>?' asked Yellow.
> 'Yes and no,' he answered. 'What <u>looks</u> like you will die but what's <u>really</u> you will still live. Life is changed, not taken away. Isn't that different from those who die without ever becoming butterflies?'

24 August 2013

Iread somewhere about Kintsugi. In Japan, if an object breaks, instead of turfing it out they often fill the cracks with gold. They believe that if something has suffered damage and has history, it becomes more beautiful, and the crack doesn't weaken the object but makes it stronger. How awesome is that?

Perfection is such a sham. I'm having such fun building our new imperfect home. I am fairly convinced that the architect thinks I'm certifiably insane, as I veer completely off his plan. Me and my trusty builder sidekick Joseph. 'Can you knock a hole in that for me, Joseph? About so big.' I will gesture with my hands to indicate the size. All very scientific. I come back with second-hand treasures, and the windows in certain rooms don't match. But that's what makes it beautiful, and what makes it ours.

It's the same with people, you know. Why pretend to be perfect when we're all deeply flawed in one way or another? Yet our 'imperfections' are the things that those who love us understand and value. Hubby, for instance, drives me crazy with his unshakeable, unchangeable little habits. Must be the Austrian blood. He will only use one kind of toothbrush. It has to be Jordan and it has to be the hard one. I suspect they stopped producing these years ago when every dentist in the world agreed that hard bristles are bad for your gums. But nay, no other toothbrush will do. I have to trawl old shops and general dealers in the hopes of locating one. But if I ever lost him, I'm sure one of the things I'd miss most is the delight I feel when I find a Jordan hard toothbrush.

I am deeply flawed, and I am broken, as we all are in one way or another. But even my friends have woken up to something. If something really good happens, like finding the perfect parking spot on a busy Saturday, they'll casually say something like 'Nice work, Sam.'

The more I speak and write about you and ensure that you remain in our lives and a part of our family, the more I can feel my cracks filling up with gold.

26 August 2013

I missed my regular writing day last week. And I really shouldn't have. It's not good for me. I tried writing at work, but with so many people around it's not possible. To write, I have to go deep inside myself and connect with Sam. This is his story as much as it's mine.

I went to see my dear friend M today, she of the glorious coloured oils. I have a bottle of Platinum Om to bath in and I can't wait. It's blue and sparkly and exactly the colour of Sam.

M has been more than a friend, though. She is more of a mentor to guide me through the changes. I met her not long before Sam passed, and the day after it happened I went to see her. I hardly remember going there. My sister drove my shattered, broken body there at my request. I somehow needed to go to her. I felt that only she could answer the burning question. The only question.

'Where *are* you, Sam?'

The answer is, 'I'm here with you, Mommy. I'm safe and warm and happy.'

M entered my life at exactly the right moment. When the student is ready, the teacher will come. Every person who enters your life has a purpose. Even those that cause you hurt – they too have their lesson to teach you and their own lesson to learn.

This became very clear to me because of a woman I will call E.

E was my nanny, but also an important teacher in my life. She arrived like a Godsend when I was pregnant with Sam. She swept in and took charge. She was bossy and opinionated, and I was fecking terrified of her. She took over my kitchen. She took over my kids. After Sam was born I was in a bad way, I can tell you. Although I managed to keep my corpse-like grin for most of the public, I was *clearly* suffering from severe postnatal depression. After three kids in five years and only about five minutes maternity leave, it should be a great surprise if you're *not* fucking depressed. Every chance I got I crept into my bed and slept. Sleep was the only escape I had.

I got medication, but it just wasn't enough. I was broken inside and had never given any time to try to heal. I plodded through the days, banging away on my PC in the office, all alone, filling out forms and crappy VAT returns all day long. Some people thrive on that sort of thing, and for them the peace and structure of office work is perfect. But I, dear friends, am no such person.

I couldn't write, and hadn't put pen to paper for ages. I had too much wine too often. I loved all my boys fiercely, but it was all very hard, you understand. E saw me through that time, and I loved her. My boys loved her. She trained in ABA therapy and became Jack's tutor. I relied on her completely.

When Sam had just turned one she simply left. She borrowed money for a holiday back home, got on a bus and never came back. I was frantic. Such a good woman with such high morals, a very vocal woman of God, would never do such a thing! I felt sure she was in trouble: hurt, injured or dead. I phoned the Consulate in Zimbabwe countless times. I phoned her family. Eventually, through endless searching, I tracked her down in Cape Town. She had simply found a new job and a boyfriend and moved on. I was devastated. It really is true that going to church doesn't make you a Christian any more than standing in a garage makes you a car.

As you can tell, I have forgiven her. Well, I'm in the process of forgiving her, which is a start. The truth is, she fulfilled a role in my life and she left when I needed her to, although I didn't realise it then. It was time for me to take back my home, my power and my children. Because I am the Mother. And I had started to crawl my way back to me.

Thank God she left when she did, or I may not really have had those six months with you, Sam. To get to know you properly and to know how clever and funny and loving you were. Are.

Forgiveness. Such a simple word for such a vast and complicated act. When you begin to know yourself, to spend time looking at what it is that is holding you back, you will need to forgive. Forgive those who hurt you, accept the lessons they offered in your life and be grateful for them. Forgive yourself for your own wrongdoings; for these too, were part of the plan.

I have said before that I believe your thoughts create your reality, and this I do not doubt. It sounds so simple though; surely if that were the case we'd all be living the perfect life by now? But the trick is finding out what those thoughts are – the real ones, often hidden deep inside you, that make you feel small, insecure, unworthy and scared. Once you uncover them, you have to work through them in your own way to release them.

And for me, a part of this process is writing, and this blog. So I know what my next topic must be, and it's not an easy one. But I will do it, Sam. I will do it for you.

27 August 2013

A few weeks ago, I went walking at Platbos. I walked the labyrinth without any thought or intention. As I stepped out I knew exactly what I needed to do. 'I need to start a blog,' I said to my friend C. The details of what it would be about were still sketchy, but I knew what I needed to do. I never imagined at that point that I would use these journals as my blog. I was still too scared to think of putting this deeply personal journey out there.

A few weeks earlier, I had met S, a new friend, blogger and spiritual warrior. Having had a stroke at a very young age, she has realised the value of life and of living at a pace that is comfortable for you. For no reason or reward she offered to help me start a blog. She showed me how it works, set it up and helped me launch (birth?) it into the wide blue yonder. It's not the most tech-savvy blog you'll ever see, but it's mine and I love it. I've been blogging for two weeks and had nearly 11 000 visitors. Better still, I've had comments and messages.

It means so much to know that our journey can and will help others, Sam. What you are teaching us is so powerful, and finally I have a way to get it out there.

28 August 2013

I have never dreamt of Sam since he left. I have thought of him often before falling asleep, in the hopes that he would be able to visit me in my dream. But I am obviously not ready yet. Seeing his little face right now might be too much for me, and bring me pain instead of the comfort he would like me to feel.

But two nights ago I saw him. Just the back of him, in his favourite khaki green sweater, running up the grass hill behind our house. I know this means I'm getting closer. Soon he will turn around and smile at me, and I'll know beyond a shadow of doubt that he's okay. I can't wait to see you, my angel boy.

1 September 2013

Synchronicity. Sensible Sister was watching a sports match at her children's school. She chatted to another mother, told her about Sam and the blog and then sent the link to her smartphone. Naturally, she is the Publishing Director of a South African publishing house. She read the blog and we set up a meeting for coffee. They would like to publish the book version of my blog. There you go. As simple and as amazing as that.

It's clear to me that Sam's blessings continue to rain down on us. It's wonderful to have such a strong spirit on our side.

My friend MJ is fond of saying that every life has a soundtrack. And it's true. Music can be very powerful and motivational. Whenever I start doubting myself, my writing and the journey I'm sharing so openly, I currently blare 'Brave' by Sara Bareilles. Cheesy as it may be, it really helps me continue.

Say what you wanna say
And let the words fall out
Honestly I wanna see you be brave

During my sabbatical, I listened to a lot of music and read a lot of motivational quotes. My brother and I also shared endless links to motivational clips. Surrounding yourself with only positive, uplifting words gradually builds you up. Similarly, you need to look at who you surround yourself with. Be careful of spending too much time and energy on people who drain you rather than building you and giving you strength.

It's a widely accepted fact that your thoughts create your reality. Be careful with your thoughts, for they have physical power.

3 September 2013

It was my birthday yesterday. I love birthdays and plan them for weeks beforehand. It's such a great time, a fresh new start with a whole blank year in front of you to plan and dream about.

This year I didn't plan a party. I've had enough parties of late. Instead, I am giving myself a truly wonderful gift. This morning hubby and I are throwing our (very small) bags in the car and taking off in the general direction of the Transkei. We have five nights for our road trip, thanks to the kindly offers of help from grannies and nannies. We haven't made a booking anywhere. We have a map, some music and a full tank of diesel.

We have done everything we can work-wise to ensure that things run smoothly, and now we must trust. The roof is going onto the new house today, and when we get back, great progress will have been made.

Of course, my suitcase of parental guilt must travel along. It's not possible to leave it behind, but I am putting it on the back of the bakkie and will try not to open it too often. The boys will be fine in their own home, surrounded by people who love them. And at the end of the day, this trip will benefit them too.

What do I want for my birthday? I want to be happy. I want my family to be happy. With all the new projects and so much stress, hubby and I have been at each other's throats. Too much snapping and bitching. And if the two of us aren't working as a team, the whole show will surely fall apart. It's vital that we keep our relationship strong. What better gift to give your children than a happy home. So off we go.

When a friend suggested we go away somewhere, I nearly laughed aloud. What? We can't go away now. We're busy building a house. What about the boys? There are flowers to be picked, there is wine to be sold, there are lunches to be served. Then I thought about it. Why the hell can't we? As a couple we've been through the wringer this year. We really, really need this.

Ironic, isn't it? When you can least afford to take time off, that's when you most need to insist on it and step out of life for a while. Or else you get so caught up in the day-to-day running of your life and those hundreds of balls in the air that you completely lose sight of the big picture.

I also need to take this time to write. To sit on a beach and let it pour out of me. Because there is more to this story, and it may even get a bit crazier. But tell it I must, in all it's truth and entirety. I need this break. And when we come back in a week, my friends, you're gonna hear me roar.

4 September 2013

I'm on a road trip with hubby. The whole experience feels so right and so powerful. It reminds us that we're on a journey together.

We have driven into the heart of the Karoo, a vast and amazing semi-desert in South Africa. Just us, the radio and a bag of biltong. Occasionally we stop and fill up our water bottles at a mountain stream. I try to be present in every moment.

We drive mostly in companionable silence, each lost in our own thoughts. I warned hubby at the beginning of the trip by my tears, which are flowing pretty freely, and that's okay. They are sad and necessary tears, and they need to be released. I cry for the little earthly boy so desperately missed. I cry for us and his brothers and his grannies and grandpas and aunties and uncles and cousins and friends – for all who loved him and have shed so many tears of their own.

It is such a desperately sad thing when a child dies, such a reversal of the natural order of things. Do you know, there's not even a name for it, this thing? If you lose your parents you're an orphan; if you lose your husband you're a widow. But what is the name for us, the broken ones? There isn't one, because people can't accept that it should happen.

5 September 2013

I just watched the sun rise over the most magnificent beach in a place called Port St Johns on the Wild Coast. Hubby and I arrived here late yesterday afternoon, the end destination of our road trip together after eight hours of travelling. That may sound like a lot. But a road trip is a lot like life. Everyone is trying to get somewhere, some sort of end destination. Yet if you slow down and really enjoy the ride, it all makes much more sense. Doesn't it?

We drove through the flat, arid Karoo, then into the rolling hills of the Transkei, dotted with traditional huts in jewel-like colours. As we reached the coast, the vegetation suddenly changed to subtropical forests of gnarled, ancient trees against craggy mountainsides. This place just blows me away.

In this particular little bay there are frequent reports of drownings. The sea is wild and unpredictable. There have been eight shark attacks in the past few years, seven of which were fatal. But truly, that's the magnificent thing about the Wild Coast. It still belongs more to nature than to man. And that is rare.

Lately, all over the news, seemingly everywhere I turn, there are stories of rape and abuse of children. It assails my senses. Yesterday, on the radio, I heard about another girl raped. Four years old! What the hell is wrong with our world?

Today, an article about child pornography in a local magazine gave this quote from the national coordinator of Childline: 'If after several years, they do succeed in identifying a child, it often causes further trauma. By then the child may have tried to process the incident and forgotten about it, and when it's exposed they or their family feel humiliated all over again.'

There is so much wrong with this statement. (a) No, the child has *not* forgotten about the incident. Rape or abuse is an attack on the spirit, the very essence of a person. It is destroying the innocence of our most precious possession, our children, and therefore our society. (b) Why should the child and family feel humiliated? The child was a victim, for God's sake. But the culture of shame around the topic continues the cycle.

I have been backwards and forwards in my own mind as to whether to blog anything about sexual abuse. It's somehow a different level of reveal, and the socially silenced little part of me says *shh,* it's too much.

But why do I still feel shame? If I am too ashamed to talk about it, how can I expect my children to open up to me if something happens to them? Maybe if I write about it I can finally let it go.

The story, sadly, is by no means unique to me. I don't remember many details of my abuse, nor of the perpetrator. Personally those details don't matter too much to me. A family member of a housekeeper, if I remember correctly. What I do remember is how it made me feel: guilty and deeply ashamed. This guilt and shame penetrated my psyche and buried itself snugly deep inside. For years I had flashbacks, and as I got older I felt quite pleased that I had overcome this horrible memory without any ill effects.

But during my time of desperate searching it kept coming up. Guilt and shame. I needed to address it. To forgive the abuser, but more importantly, to forgive myself. And we all need to talk about it, to be open with ourselves and our children. Because this shit needs to stop. It was not my fault; I am innocent. Keep saying this until your heart truly accepts it.

If we want to stop it we need to treat the cause. What is it? Is it an illness? If it is, are we searching for a cure? Bipolar disorder, schizophrenia and many other disorders can be properly managed through medication. Why not these abnormal and damaging sexual urges? The chances are that the abuser was also abused as a child. One abuser grows up and abuses three. Of those three, two grow up and abuse three each... You get the picture.

We need to break the cycle of shame by saying out loud that which is unmentionable. If someone feels the urge, they should be allowed free and anonymous treatment, through medication and therapy, until they are healed.

It is a sickness that can spread, and we need to deal with it openly and provide help for both victims and perpetrators.

My very wise therapist L, in a different conversation, once used the story of Rumpelstiltskin to illustrate a point to me. In the story, the evil little man gives the heroine three days to guess his name, or he will take her firstborn baby. On day three (when she has in fact overheard the real name somewhere) he comes again. 'What's my name, what's my name?' he cries, rubbing his hands in anticipatory glee. 'Rumpelstiltskin!' she shouts, 'Rumpelstiltskin, Rumpelstiltskin!' At which point, the bad guy shrieks in utter despair, tears himself in two and disappears.

The point to the story is that once you give something a name, it loses all power over you. Nameless fears, once openly identified, can be dealt with.

Rumple-fucking-*stiltskin*, people! Let's call it by its name.

6 September 2013

We had freshly opened oysters for breakfast this morning, bought from a passing fisherman. We spent the morning walking on the beach, just at the edge of the foamy water. We clambered over a small mountain of rocks and came across a beautiful tidal pool in the centre. Not a soul was around, so we stripped off and swam in the aquamarine water. There were flat rocks perfectly submerged under the surface to lounge on. Smaller flat rocks made a natural staircase in and out of the water. I have never seen or experienced a more beautiful pool, not in the best hotels I've seen. I'm reminded of that LGT... it's the simple things.

We came back to our little room on the beach and slept with the doors wide open, the crashing of the waves loud in our ears. It's good that we've come here, where nature is so powerful. We needed this trip to heal our relationship, each other and ourselves.

Of course, we think and speak of Sam and our other boys, and we phone the boys at home every day. It's been so sweet and strange to speak to them. They sound fine and happy. 'Are you having a nice holiday, Mommy?' asks Alex. 'Hello, my mommy. I'm miss you,' says Jack cheerfully. They sound so grown up and the invisible umbilical cord tugs. To be having a meaningful conversation with Jack on the phone is a miracle. I am loving every minute of this break, yet I can't wait to get home.

15 September 2013

I've been struggling to blog. I am able to write, but putting it out there is so scary sometimes. Will people judge me? Today is my old friend C's birthday. She lives in New Zealand now. We've known each other since we were fourteen, and we've been through loads of shit together. I wrote her a mail – it was easy. Then I realised I have to do the same with this blog: treat it as though I'm writing to an old friend. Because it's my hope, as always, that it reaches those who need it, for whatever reason of their own.

My dear C!!
Happiest of happies to you on your birthday. Hope you are having most marvellous fun. Miss you loads. When you coming to SA? What a *mindfuck* of a year, much of it devastating and then much of it positive. Things are going well here. Am crazy as a loon. Do meditations, affirmations, use colour therapy oils. Use tarot cards and colour cards and crystals. Kinesiology, reiki, talk to self in mirror using only positive words. Switch my phone off and disappear for hours on end. Am doing a Heal Your Life course once a week with other loons, who are all perfectly lovely and sane. Because on some level I feel saner than I ever have. I miss Sam dreadfully, often and devastatingly. We all do. Not just me, but brothers and fathers and grannies and grandpas and aunties and uncles and cousins and friends. No-one will ever forget the sadness we have all been through.

And it is deep. Yet there is a joy in my life now, which was missing before, and that is because of Sam.

I am writing, and you know that is good for me. Writing up a storm, but sometimes it's very hard to push 'publish' and put it all out there, and some days I just can't. But then I get a message, some sort of cosmic shove that tells me it's okay, I am on the right track, and this process is right and good for me. That life is indeed unfolding as it should, and as it was always meant to. I just need to trust the process.

The kids are really doing well. Today is hard, because Jack's puppy Sheila is missing. Another dog came for a walk on the farm with its owner, and the two of them ran off together. That was on Friday, and no sign of them since. Have phoned neighbouring farmers, and vets and kennels are aware. What else to do? We are keeping him distracted as he is helping at the restaurant today, which is totally his favourite thing. But we are all very bleak and worried. The kids don't need this now, but can you really protect them from the fragility and unpredictability of life? I am just keeping a very positive attitude, and am sure she will come home soon. Alex had a cry about Sam yesterday for the first time in a while, and I think the crying together did us good. He said, 'I just want to give him a kiss and a cuddle.' It is fairly heart breaking, but after a cry we get up and do something happy. And every day there is more happy and less sad.

Don't know if you have seen my blog? Crazybutterflylady. wordpress.com

Haven't blogged for a while, I have had a bit of confidence wobble. But will spray myself with some hard pear tree essence, meditate with some lovely crystals, and make myself strong again. I read the book you gave me, *Seven Spiritual Laws of Success*, quite often. And love reading *Unstoppable Me*, the book you sent for the kids. Thank God for self-help books, the combination of all of them has saved my life, I think.

I am reading a book now called *Dark Night of the Soul*. It

makes loads of sense. We all have them, these soul-changing challenges. And we have to go through them, and if we use them correctly they bring about positive and necessary changes in ourselves, which make us better people. I went to visit our friend T the other day, on our road trip. I haven't seen her since she was diagnosed with breast cancer. She has finished her chemo for now, and to me her shaved head makes her look just like a warrior. And she is so strong and positive, and more peaceful than I have seen her in years.

We had long chats and loads of laughs, and it felt so good to see her. I read somewhere about the process by which a butterfly hatches. The caterpillar makes its cocoon and goes inside and comes out a butterfly. But if you open the cocoon half way you will not find any kind of animal, but a sort of butterfly mush. The whole being dissolves and then is totally reformed in a different shape. Something has to die to give way to something new. And we decided, T and I, that is where we are now. We are a kind of butterfly mush. But luckily the story of the butterfly always has a happy ending.

I love you my old friend, and miss you loads.
All my love Jami xxxx

17 September 2013

What an amazing couple of days. I was having such a wobble. I could feel my strength waning. A poor customer and dear friend commented on Sunday that I've lost so much weight, and I made a sarky comment and promptly burst into tears. Most alarming for people paying good money to come for lunch and be treated to a grief-stricken crazy lady display. And I know it's okay to cry sometimes, and I often do, but really, there's a time and a place.

I have lost weight. My jeans fall off me. I still struggle to eat. Food holds no appeal. But I force myself, because I need the strength. I have gone grey. I suddenly noticed the other day a patch of grey in hubby's eyebrow. I don't mind, I think it's cute. But this world has taken its toll on us, and our wrinkles and frown lines and sagging necks are battle scars from the story of life.

Yesterday I had a very, very blue Monday. Depressed, tearful and missing you, my boy. I drew a card and the message was 'Ask for what you want'. So last night I took a long bath, with incense, oils and a special blue candle. And I spoke to you, and to God, and to all my angels, and asked for help.

And today I got a call from the publishers that have expressed an interest in publishing my story as a book. And it's definite, they want to publish it next year. And instantly my connection strengthened again. You and I know that this is the path for our story, Sam, that this is our purpose. Thank you for proving to me once again that it's all true. Every word.

This story must be told, so let's take the leap, shall we?

So many people have mentioned a book to me called *Many Lives, Many Masters*. It kept coming up in my life. On Sunday I found my long-lost Kindle while organising some stuff. Aah, the luxury of a bookshop at your fingertips. So I charged it and downloaded the book. But, alas, at bedtime I discovered I had somehow downloaded the audio version only. Yet so determined was I that I simply lay down and pressed play. Hubby was already half-asleep next to me, and cocked his eye slightly at me as a voice started coming out of my book talking about past lives. I'm sure his 'God, she's gone loony' antenna were quivering wildly.

But something resonated powerfully with me, and this morning life is clear again. I know now what the next step is.

27 September 2013

I have been going through a tough time. I have been unable to write. I have not been spending enough time with my children. I have not been giving enough time to my marriage. I have not been taking enough time for myself. It's like an insidious, progressive illness. I get it under control and then gradually it builds up, and I find myself becoming raw, ragged and weak. Too much time at work spent with so many people around me. Running from one thing to the next at breakneck speed. A constant nagging anxiety, because there's just *not enough time!* But I've been here before, and at least this time I know what to do. I need to retreat, immediately and without apology.

Once in the past, when I got to this stage, my friend P gave me some animal cards to play with. The card I drew for my present was the Opossum (retreats, plays dead) and the card I drew for my future was the Badger (the power of the badger lies in its aggressiveness and willingness to fight for what it wants). I think sometimes we all need our Opossum time in order to unleash our inner Badgers on the world. Or something like that.

I need to make myself strong again now, and already it's working. I need to give myself time alone, and time to connect with Sam. And I need to be home with my family.

We all do it; we overcommit ourselves constantly and then strip ourselves bare in the process. Just say no... the people who care about you will understand.

So I find myself here on a Friday night, in my gown in front of the fire, watching *Cat in the Hat* with my boys. And right now, I can't think of anywhere in the world I would rather be.

I've taken a couple of days off and created for myself a cosy office in a secret location (secret to my kids as yet, anyway). And I have begun my scribbles again. Such a relief. I've been so stuck, and I know it was the reality of publishing a book that shocked me into immobility. But I've had time to listen to my heart these last few days, and I remember now. It's not about a frigging book. It never was. I write, because I have to. My task is to get the message of Sam and God and the angels and butterflies out there. The only thing that can bring me the peace I so desperately crave is to follow this path and honour our journey, Sam. Writing is good, but I also need to share it, because out there somewhere are people who will finally know they're not alone.

So I will keep blogging and putting it out there. It may not be every day, but I will do my utmost to keep it more regular. This very evening I drew an animal card, and it was the Unicorn. So true for me right now, but also for all of us.

UNICORN

Whatever the artistic vehicle through which you express your most creative self, make it a priority in your life by devoting some time, energy and perhaps even money towards this artistic pursuit. Let the longing of your heart determine what the form of your imaginative expression is, but let it be one that elicits passion and purpose. Allow it to evolve as needed, without acceding to any internal perfectionism about the end product. The process itself is where the magic is, let that alone be your satisfaction and delight.

28 September 2013

Two people asked my advice yesterday on what they should say to friends who have lost a child. I really struggled to answer them. What do I know? I know only my own experience. I am not qualified to give guidance on the experience of others. But I can share what helped me, and I hope that will be good enough.

Nothing you can say to a grieving parent will bring them instant comfort. Nothing at all. Not while the pain is so intense and so raw that you feel you will never recover. Just be there, be available, be a shoulder to cry on. Let them know you're there for them, but keep your distance enough to allow them the space to grieve. Surround them as much as possible with love and practical support, to ensure they have no cares or worries other than surviving the loss. As they begin to 'come round' (the only way I can think of to describe re-entry into the world after the first few days of shock) make sure they have all their physical needs met.

The only thing that can get you through something like this, in my opinion, is faith. Faith in whatever makes sense to you, and to those affected by the passing. For some that means church, the Bible and prayer, and that is a good way. Some people are more sceptical about traditional religion, but still, if they dig deep, they can discover their own faith. The details of my faith may differ from yours, but in the end it all leads to the same place. And that place is God, source, creator and eternal power.

I couldn't lift my heavy shoes some days if it wasn't for my solid belief that I will see Sam again and that this is all part of a much bigger picture than we can currently imagine.

I always had vague faith, but in my broken state I discovered my true belief. It's not that I don't believe in Jesus, you see, I'm still figuring it all out. But I believe in God and in goodness, and I sure as shit believe in the afterlife.

In the days following Sam's passing (and yes, I do believe that passing is a more accurate description than death) I lay on the couch like a corpse. Arty Sister sat beside me and wiped my tears constantly with a damp cloth. Mom and friends brought endless cups of tea and regular tranquilisers and cigarettes and food that would not be eaten. Sensible Sister brought me books. Lots and lots of books, all relating to people's experiences of life after death, and the wonder that awaits us when we pass from this world to the next.

There are hundreds of these books, literally hundreds. Why would so many people bother to make this shit up? And what interests me is that more and more professionals respected in their fields are coming forward with their own experiences – established doctors, psychiatrists and scientists, risking their credibility and no doubt experiencing much ridicule among their peers.

Take them books, the grieving parents. I didn't just read them; I devoured them. I was so desperate for reassurance and I needed to know that it was true. And the more I came to believe it, the more proof I saw and felt and recognised in my own life. That has been my saving grace. Sam is not gone, although we miss his physical presence every day. He is here with us and around us, and one day we will all be together again. And as long as I remember that, and stay connected, there is always a bright, warm light at the end of this tunnel, no matter how long and deep and dark it feels.

Some of the books that helped are more traditionally Christian, and some are written by more loony medium types.

But the core message is the same.

> Lisa Williams, *The Survival of the Soul*
> Don Piper, *90 Minutes in Heaven*
> Elissa Al-Chokhachy, *Our Children Live On*
> Mia Dolan, *The Gift*
> Todd Burpo, *Heaven is for Real*
> Rebecca Springer, *Within Heaven's Gates*
> Roberts Liardon, *Visions of Heaven*
> Dr Gerald G May, *The Dark Night of the Soul*
> Dr Eben Alexander, *Proof of Heaven*
> Dr Brian L Weiss, *Many Lives, Many Masters*

How can all these people be exactly the same kind of crazy? I cry for all those parents and their unique and unbearable pain. And I pray that they will believe.

6 October 2013

This week I spent a morning with Jack at the hospital, having grommets inserted into his ears. This is the third pair, so you'd think I'd be pretty much an expert. But I hate it. Holding that plastic mask over his mouth and nose while he struggles until he falls asleep... The doctors swear he won't remember any of it, but how the hell do they know for sure? It feels like such a betrayal of my boy. Waking up from the anaesthetic is also fairly traumatic, as many mothers of young kids will testify. The thrashing and screaming, apparently a natural reaction.

It makes me wonder once again... who the hell would voluntarily sign up for this hair-raising ride of parenthood? I read somewhere once that having a child is like deciding to allow your heart to walk around outside your body for the rest of your life. But afterwards, cuddling him in his little hospital gown for two hours, I remembered why. I have lost one child, and nothing will ever take away that pain. But the real point, I think, is to treasure our children every moment. Feel that cuddle, and the love behind it, with your whole heart and being.

On Tuesday I lit a candle for Sam, and I asked Alex if he would like to send a message. At the mention of Sam's name he usually stops what he's doing immediately, and quite a sad and tearful communication to his little brother follows. But this time he carried on playing, and said very casually, 'Not right now, thanks, I'm busy.' In a way that was very sad, and in another way it is wonderful to see my beautiful boy start to rebuild his heart. It's as though Sam is giving us all permission to be okay and carry on.

Our new house is so nearly ready, just frustrating details to go. We are making it so super special for the boys, with their built-in bunk beds and racetrack linoleum floor. They have been through so much this year – we all have – and this move needs to be the happiest memory ever. Change is hard sometimes, but learning to accept and embrace it is an important part of growing.

11 October 2013

It's 5:30 am and still dark outside. Everyone is sleeping, and I can hear the cry of our resident wild peacock, which means the sun will soon be up. So will the rest of the world. But for now, I'm just enjoying the feeling of having the world pretty much to myself for an hour, in my gown at my laptop with a hot cup of coffee.

I am currently reading *The Power of Now* by Eckhart Tolle. I can't believe I've only discovered it recently when it's been around for years. It makes so much sense to me. We are all so concerned with our mistakes from the past and our desires and fears for the future, that we often overlook the fact that what really matters is *now* – this minute, this second. As I sit here I am safe, secure and happy, and all my needs are met. Sure, the day will bring its problems, but I will deal with them one by one as they arrive, and each will be manageable. But for now, this room is warm, this coffee is delicious and life is pretty grand.

My hands are all spattered with paint. Our new house is so close to ready, and we've been working late evenings and weekends to get it done. It's more than a new home; it represents so much to our family. A fresh start, a clean slate, a new beginning. The contractors still look at me suspiciously, as though I'm a strange creature from a distant land. Yesterday, when I asked the carpenter to nail an old suitcase to the wall and build shelves in it, I think he nearly called for the mental health professionals.

But I love every corner of our home, built entirely from leftover materials on the farm, using old pallets and fruit bins for shelving wherever possible. My paintwork is probably not the most professional you've seen. As I was painting over a large gouge in the wall yesterday, I felt the eyes of hubby over my shoulder, trying his best to bite his tongue regarding my lack of wall preparation. But as I explained to him, perfection is so boring. That's the look everyone goes for, isn't it? Why not try something different? My system is just fine, thank you. One little dead spider may take only one coat of paint to cover, while a larger insect in my way takes two or three coats, depending on its size.

By next week we will be moving in. I am taking down the board that points to the house today. It used to say *Manager*, but I intend to sand it down and paint *Private*. Or *Fuck Off We're Busy*. Or something like that.

We have been furiously packing up various rooms in the house each night. For every box that will travel with us, at least two boxes will not. I intend to travel light, both physically and mentally. Sadly, hubby is something of a hoarder, so much of his stuff will need to be thrown away in secret. Our current hermit status is helped along by our commitment to a Sober October. Not a drop of alcohol has passed our lips, which, if you know us, is something of a miracle. It's both harder and easier than I thought. Easy while I'm home playing puzzles with the kids, and harder if I'm at a party.

This means that in the past eleven days I've spent a lot of time playing puzzles and hardly any time at parties. It's about more than giving up the booze, I guess, and more of a commitment to my children and husband. In effect, I am nesting. Preparing to move our family to our new nest built from sticks, spittle and love.

And we can't wait. So blogging has been relegated to the sidelines until we're safely in our new home.

The sun is coming up, the birds have started singing and I

am waiting to hear Boy One's morning call. 'Good morning, mommy. I is very hungry.' Then I shall have to go and drag Boy Two moaning from his bed. 'But I'm still *tired.*' And I will love every minute of it, this life, with all its work and worries and schedules. Because that is the decision I have made, to be happy in the now.

I am ready to carpe the shit out of this diem. And you will be hearing from me soon.

22 October 2013

I'm up at the crack of dawn because I can't sleep. It's moving day today. Real, actual moving day. I have waited so long to get into our new house. Now it's actually happening.

Sometimes life feels so unreal. I have come to realise that the pace of life we've become accustomed to is not natural or healthy. There have been times when I've had to change the ringtone on my cell phone to try to combat the jarring stress I feel each time it rings. Sometimes I hear phantom vibrations and I'm sure it's a phone ringing. It's not healthy to be contactable *one hundred percent* of the time. No wonder we all feel so frazzled.

My phone battery died on Friday, and I only bothered to charge it again on Monday. Has the country's economy come to a grinding halt? Probably, but I can't be blamed for that. As I haven't looked at a newspaper, I wouldn't know if it had. Was there a drastic emergency like running out of ice during lunch service? If there was, I'm sure it was ably handled. I, however, was filling up my soul spending time with friends. Great and wonderful friends, and especially great girlfriends. God, women are fantastic. Men are wonderful too (mostly), but women are different. We are so much more open and willing to share our scars and our stories, and through that, helping to heal each other.

We have changed so much, this old group of friends. We have been through sickness, pain, death, parenting and grief. We're all the same, yet completely different. And this year, in particular, has been a doozy. 2013. Thirteen is a karmic number, the number of upheaval so that new ground can be broken.

I lost one of my children. The one thing I knew for sure I could never survive. Yet here I am, surviving it. A strength has entered my heart through faith. Faith that there is a grand plan in place and that my journey through life continues with all three of my sons at my side, although it will always hurt that I can only hold two of them.

I have still not dreamt of Sam. I have thought of him while falling asleep in the hopes that he will come. I have sprayed my pillow with all manner of potions. But nada. Recently, though, I have felt him. Last week I went to the big city to buy some stuff for the new house. (So much fun. Ridiculously fun. Should be illegal.) I was, as I always am, very aware that my boys were in the back of the car, although they were quiet. I dropped them off at school, kissed them goodbye and got back into the car. For the rest of the drive I remained intensely aware that I still had a child on the back seat. I felt him so strongly, and it felt so comforting.

Then last Friday I felt an urge to go into Sam's garden, where I sat down on the earth and wrote him a letter. A big orange and black butterfly came and flitted around me as I wrote, and stayed with me. Sam. Sam. Sam. He is so powerful.

I had a conversation not long ago with an elderly man who recently lost his wife. 'I'm doing okay,' he said to me. 'But sometimes, like today, I am thinking of her when one of our favourite songs comes on the radio. It makes me so sad.' I said to him, 'That can make you sad, but that's also when you should feel your happiest. Because it's no coincidence, it's a message from your wife. Look out for the signs, and they will come.'

This week I was contacted by someone I know from school. A lovely girl, but not someone I knew well. Her father passed away recently, and her mother had been to see a medium called T who really helped her. She wanted to give me a gift, a session with this woman. I accepted, because accepting gifts is part of realising that everything happens for a reason.

So today at 10 am I have my appointment, in between hanging curtains and unpacking boxes. I'm expecting nothing, truly. But I will go with an open mind and an open heart to learn more lessons. And I can't wait.

Hubby just woke up and found me dressed and raring to go. 'It's moving day!' I declared joyfully. There are still a number of details to take care of, and hubby looked at me sleepily and said, 'We don't *have* to move today, you know.'

Is he mental? I have such joy and excitement and delight in my heart today, and tonight I plan to sleep in our New Home! I have waited for what seems like forever for this day, and I will not wait a moment longer. Even if our bedroom floor could use another coat of paint.

10 pm

What did I learn from the reading? I'll let you decide. Here are my handwritten notes as I recorded them.

Who would you like me to call?
Call Sam.
Do you have three children? Or is it two? I see one of them being around more.
I had three. We lost one, and that is Sam.
Ah. Your father says something about a watch that isn't working. You have to get it working again. It was his, and always on him; a special item. Get it fixed.
Sam's passing difficult to deal with, emotions shut down. Is it two boys you still have?
Yes.
Rough journey you're on. Sam is coming through. He's older now, thirteen or fourteen. It's easier for him to communicate that way than as a baby. He says he arrived out of the blue, unplanned, but felt completely loved and welcomed.
There is stuff going down his throat that shouldn't be there.

He drowned.

He loves you so much, and his brothers and his dad. He is very emotional. You had warned him not to go there but still he went. Was it your pool at home? He shows me the other two swimming and you would take him in.

He loved water, a complete water baby, he was fascinated with it. You had caught him alone at the pool before and warned him.

He shows himself as being two-ish, a strong-willed little guy. He doesn't know how to describe it, but he needed to go to the water. You were quick to find him, but it was still too late. It's very hard not to blame yourself and others. Was the gate left open? He shows that he walked straight through. It was very quick, wasn't it?

You'd put him in a room with lots of toys and he went out again.

There was no panic; it was a peaceful passing. That's why you didn't hear anything.

He felt very loved, and is still very much around your family. He feels sadness because he makes you sad.

Are you considering selling your home?

We're moving soon.

Good, you need to move. It will be a good fresh start, and re-energise all of you. You need a sense of your space.

Cut yourself some slack, go at your own pace. It's okay to accept that the grief will be lifelong. Lots of friends and family who want to support you.

Moving on does not mean forgetting about him. You beat yourself up day and night. Stop; be kind to yourself. It's going to take time. Watch out for depression, which leads to non-function. If not for the other boys, you wouldn't get out of bed. See them as your strength and not your weakness. Take ̶ ̶t: *stop rushing. Write to him every day, it will help you*

still got Sam's ashes?

Yes.

Keep them at the new house like you've wanted to. I see a bed of flowers, a stone and a place to go and speak to him. Writing is a huge healing tool for you, but you already know that.

Remember him and speak about him. It will help you to move on and bring you together.

Did you get a puppy?

Yes, but she ran away.

I see you have a big plot. It's easy to gain access outside. She's in a nearby township; someone has adopted her. You've phoned all the vets but had no word. She's not dead, but a lovely looking dog, so someone has kept her.

She was a gap filler, to bring some joy into the house. She says she's unlikely to return. Her breed is known for running away. Look at other dogs. She brought so much joy. Give it a bit more time and then get a new dog.

Keep lighting candles and keeping a space for Sam. He likes that. Going to take time, don't try to do everything at once. Focus on the good; you are the key figure to get them through. Don't hide your grief from your husband and children.

26 October 2013

Please make us strong, Sam. This is a home of happiness and joy; let us feel you here. Today is very emotional. I am so enjoying packing out pretty things in our new home, and arranging the boys' toys. The boys *love* their construction themed bathroom and their racetrack floors.

But you should be here with us. The five of us. You would have so loved this. Instead, we had to bring your ashes, our darling angel son and brother. The heaviest box I have ever carried. All that is left of the earthly being so treasured by us all. It's brutal and it's vicious and the utter cruelty of it seems unbearable sometimes. And this week has brought a lot of tears. But then I go into a very still space, and I feel you again and feel your love surround me. And the hurt eases. It's a gentler aching pain; not the scary, stabbing pain of the first months. I need to accept that it will never go away, and that this grieving will be a lifelong process.

Yet, as I sit here this morning, still in my gown in my peaceful new home, with Saturday morning cartoons and Milo in the background, I am completely content and at peace. It really feels like we've come home.

I suspect this may be my last blog for a while. It is time for me to focus on the book, the next chapter of this mysterious and ing called life. It will be published during the second ear, all going according to plan. What have I learnt? rnt that this is *my* life, and the pace I choose to live it at is nobody's decision but mine.

I have learnt to say no. Just no. So much of my life before this was spent saying yes to the needs of everyone else that I barely had time for the things that really matter. A while ago an ex-committee colleague called to ask if I would like to help organise certain aspects of an upcoming village event. I gleefully said no. In fact, if memory serves, I told him I would rather stay home and stick needles in my eyes. It felt great, and I'm really proud of myself. Since then I joyfully blurt out the word at every opportunity. Can you help us with this? *No!* Can you arrange that? *No!* Can you be available for this? *No, I fucking won't!* It's a fairly childish and unrealistic way to live, but I'm sure I'll grow out of it, and hopefully at the end there will be some balance. But for now, I make no excuses for wanting to spend my time at home with my family, who are my blessing and my strength. And this lesson is because of you, Sam.

Even after Sam left, my instinct was to start running and never stop. I organised a big wedding during March, and I was in danger of slipping straight back into my old patterns. At the wedding, I tore the ligaments in my ankle, and I couldn't walk for two weeks. A sign. The ankle was starting to heal when I ran into someone in the local supermarket. 'We really miss you on such-and-such committee,' he said. And being The One Who Says Yes, I replied, 'I think I'm almost ready to come back.'

Straight afterwards I went to a physiotherapist appointment a friend had made for me, insisting that the ankle needed professional treatment. I walked up the stairs and saw her logo on the front door, the windows, the walls. A big purple butterfly! Sam's message was like a slap in the face. 'Are you crazy, Mommy? Have I taught you *nothing*? Slow down, Mommy, *slow down*.'

I came back and sent out a few emails, resigning from any external time-thief commitments. I focused on my own business and my family. Now my business has begun to thrive, and so has my family. So have I.

It's been a crazy busy week, what with moving home. But I've taken time out. I dropped the boys at school and went to spend time next to the sea with a takeaway coffee. Forty minutes was enough soul filling to see me through the rest of the day. Aside from a school concert, I've barely left the house.

I have learnt that the small things really matter a lot. In my new home I have a kettle that whistles. It makes me so happy. And hubby has a shaving mirror in the shower that extends on an arm, an odd but endearing personal dream. A good book, a glass of nice wine, a hot bath... These are wonderful things if you are present for them and savour the moment.

I have learnt that my own time is the most valuable thing I own, and I should be careful how I spend it. This week I have baked rolls, cooked meals, made play dough and pancakes, and still had time to do my work. That's because I have left out the extra stuff, the stuff that *really* takes up your time.

I have learnt that people are generally good. Not all of them entirely good, but everyone has good in them. Nobody is perfect, and we need to be careful how we judge others if we don't know the personal lessons they are having to learn.

I have learnt that I am married to a good man. A strong, brave man when the shit really hit the fan. And if we can get through this, we can get through anything. Although please don't think our relationship is perfect. He can be a right asshole sometimes, as I'm sure (very occasionally) so can I.

I have learnt that I need to follow my passion. I write. I am a writer. I have always known it, but the fear of not being good enough has held me back, as it does many of us. But since Sam passed, writing has been my greatest healer. Putting it out there, speaking it aloud has helped our family to re-enter the world as normal people. Yes, it's hard. Yes, it's excruciatingly painful. But you don't have to feel awkward around us, because it's okay Sam. It's vital to talk about Sam. He is not a sad powerful, wonderful blessing we were given, and be grateful and honour him by speaking his name.

I have learnt that, when it comes to your kids, you need to trust your own instincts, because *you are the mother*. The boys are both doing so well. Alex is one of the strongest and cleverest people I know. He has shown such maturity in the face of his own loss, and bravely spoken about his feelings to let them out and let himself heal. He is amazing.

I have learnt that Jack is my greatest teacher (aside from you, Sam). Having a child with special needs is a very strange and complicated journey, and, of course, at times it is extremely hard. But the boy we have raised is happy and confident and loving and loved, and isn't that the kind of child we all want?

At the school concert this week Jack was a pig and Alex a rhino. Alex was typically cool, just doing his own thing and not remotely perturbed by anyone else's activities or what he was *supposed* to be doing. Very Jack Nicholson, hubby and I agreed.

Jack was very distracted because he was scanning the audience for us. When he spotted us (me waving like a lunatic) he declared, 'Hello Mommy!', turned to someone in the wings and shouted, 'That's my mommy!' and then threw himself into the song march with gusto. But in his enthusiasm he came right out to the front of the stage, and thus when the curtain closed, he was standing there alone. He headed for the stairs and, as he still struggles a bit with steep stairs, the principal got up to help him down. From the rows in front of me I heard a murmur of sympathy. 'Ag, shame.' I wanted to leap up and shout, 'Ag shame, what? Did you not witness that performance? The child was fucking *magnificent!*' Best of all was that he loved it. Hubby and I went backstage to collect the boys and Jack was grinning from ear to ear. 'Is you so ploud of me?' he asked. We are *so* frigging ploud of him.

I have learnt that you truly do not know how strong you are until being strong is the only choice you have. And that even great suffering can bring about powerful positive changes if you let it, if you look deeply inside yourself and try to find the lesson.

I have learnt that there is no such thing as death. I believe that our souls will live on and that our family will all be together again one day. On Tuesday I went for a reading with a medium, and I learnt that although Sam had to leave us, he hated to leave as much as we hated him to. That is our path together, our contract, and the love between us all is still so powerful. He shows us every day that he is there.

I have learnt that we have wonderful people in our lives. Our family, our extended family, our in-laws, our friends and our community have shown me the good in people, the very best of people, at the hardest time of our lives. And we are so grateful.

This year has changed me. I will never be the same person again. But here, in our cosy family home with my kettle just about to whistle, it feels like I can finally stop running.

Thank you, thank you, Sam-I-am.

10 November 2013

Yesterday we attended a memorial service, another one, for someone we had only recently come to know. A young man in the prime of his life. His small aircraft crashed last weekend, killing him instantly, leaving behind a wife and two beautiful children.

I thought I would be okay, but when we arrived his father was speaking, and his pain was so raw and deep that it touched my own grieving parent nerve. And I cried a very painful set of tears. I saw hubby go up to him and have a fairly long conversation, which looked quite intense. I didn't have to ask what it was about, but when hubby came back to me his eyes were sad, but somehow stronger than before. Perhaps now it will always be part of our lives to try to use our experience to help others.

Today I feel so much better. We are allowed to cry, all of us, in fact we should and we must. It is like a pressure cooker, and dipping in, opening the valve and releasing, stops me from imploding.

15 November 2013

My Darling Sam,
I am so sorry. Please forgive me.

I have been doing a colour therapy course, which I love. The thing that keeps coming up for me is forgiveness. Last night before bed I again drew the forgiveness card. I couldn't understand it. I have gone to great lengths through various methods to identify those in my life who I needed to forgive, and I have done the work to forgive them. Who is it then? Who still needs forgiveness?

This morning I was feeling pretty chirpy. Then I got a phone call.

The police need me or hubby to come in and make a statement before they can close the case on Sam's passing. It tapped on the fragile surface of the grieving mother that forever dwells in this body of mine. And she came out wailing.

'Was I negligent?' she cried, tearing at her hair. 'Was it my fault, Sam? Did you reach for me in your moment of fear and *I wasn't there?*' I've known this feeling was there, but I was afraid to touch it. But here it is, in my face. The person I need to forgive is me.

I am your mother, Sam, and I did not protect you well enough. A long time ago I put a silly cartoon on Facebook, and now it haunts me. It was a woman saying glibly, 'Of course, I'm a good mother… they're alive, aren't they?'

Ha fucking ha. Now one of them is forever gone, and what does that make me?

But clearly the next part of my journey is this – the greatest forgiveness of all, and the most difficult. But Sam will help us do it.

Hubby and I just went together to the police station. He gave the statement while I sat quietly crying. He was so strong, so matter-of-fact. But I know this is not how he feels inside; it can't be. Our baby is gone, and that fact will never change. I sent hubby off for a drive around the farm and begged him to let himself feel it, just for a few moments. Allow his heart to tear open a bit and let the grieving father cry. Because if we don't, we will never move forward with our healing. Bit by painful, heartbreaking bit we need to move forward every single day. 'Now the case can be closed,' said the kindly policeman. Jesus Christ, don't I wish it were that easy.

I'm sorry, please forgive me. I love you, thank you.

17 November 2013

Wowsers. Hair-raising stuff by anyone's standards. Yesterday it started to rain, and it hasn't stopped for one moment. This morning we woke at 4 am, and as soon as it was light enough, hubby went off into the torrential downpour to survey the damage.

It is extensive.

The weir has completely washed away, meaning that there will soon be no water in the taps. There is no telephone and there is no electricity. The farm road has disappeared under a newly formed rushing river. The main house is completely flooded, and the roads to both Hermanus and Stanford are closed due to flooding.

Did I mention that we are hosting a function today? A thirtieth birthday party for a hundred people, twenty-seven of whom arrived last night. Naturally, said guests are now physically unable to leave, as are we.

Our trusty Tasting Room gals B and L and some concerned farm workers tried every route to get to work, but the emergency vehicles wouldn't let them through. So they parked on the side of the road and walked over the fairly treacherous bridge in the rain to a section of the road where hubby could collect them.

That's what is so interesting about the way our business is developing. We're a team. Everyone has different positions, but we're all working towards the same goal. And that goal is bigger than mere money.

Trusty tractor drivers worked in the pouring rain, fixing the farm road so that access to Stanford was possible, if still difficult. The kitchen boiled big pots of mountain water on gas, and made trays of milky instant coffee for the guests, who couldn't have enjoyed them more if they were semi-skinny decaf lattes. Big pans of scrambled eggs, bread, bacon and sliced tomato were served, and the fire lit.

Quick staff meeting. Right, what shall we do? The other seventy-three expected guests will never make it here, but we're stuck with twenty-seven. The only logical thing to do is to throw the best party we know how.

A daring trip by hubby, escorted by Fire and Rescue, over the small section of remaining road leading into Stanford, shortly before it collapsed entirely. He asked the owner of the local Spar if he knew of anyone with a spare generator. Naturally, being Stanford, a kindly stranger in the next aisle did, and offered to lend it to us.

Electricity for the lights, music and smoke machine, plenty of food and booze, and in the middle of all the destruction we threw a totally kick-ass party.

And so it goes with life. Things come your way, both good and bad, and sometimes downright terrible. But there is always something to celebrate, and if you open your eyes you'll find it.

It's so important to enjoy the now, and not spend your life worrying about things that may never happen, or have happened in the past. All that counts is this moment.

20 November 2013

On Monday morning the last of the guests were able to gingerly tackle the road off the farm and back towards Cape Town. Smiling and waving, they shouted that Floodfest was the memory of a lifetime.

Hard work lies ahead to restore the damage the farm has suffered. But first, hubby and I set off on a Monday morning hiking expedition to explore the new terrain.

We hiked high into the kloof at the back of the farm, previously inaccessible due to overgrown vegetation. We clambered over huge trees and boulders washed down by the torrent, and marvelled at the power of nature. And then we sat and enjoyed the newly created waterfalls.

Yes, there is a lot of work and expense ahead. But there is also good in everything.

10 pm
Wow, it's quiet. The only sound I can hear is the wind whistling outside. It's awesome, and I appreciate every second of this silence.

It's been a bit of a crazy time of late, one of those times when life seems to be on fast forward and you're unsure how to slow it down. I suspect that finding this balance will be my great challenge in life. Finding enough time and space to keep myself sane and healthy, and still cope with the real life actually happening outside my own head.

It was building up again, and I could feel the slight unravelling beginning, as the threads holding me together started to fray around the edges. And then the floods came, and the road into the village collapsed. This meant that as of Saturday we could see our friends and neighbours and wave to them over the rushing water, but not reach them.

Really, Sam, it's a bit extreme, don't you think? Putting a giant chasm into a national road as a sign for me to retreat? I phoned N to tell her my theory. 'Jayzuz, woman, be careful with those powers of yours!' she cried, and we collapsed with laughter.

And now, my car won't start – there's some fault with the battery. And my phone's battery is also faulty and only lasts about thirty minutes before switching itself off. Is there a sign there somewhere do you think?

I am supposed to be writing. I need to write, and Sam goes to great lengths to remind me of that. But I've reached a difficult stage of the journey, with new challenges that I have to overcome. The Oprah magazine has picked up on the blog, and would like an article from me for their March issue. This is a new level of putting it out there – my whole family out in the big, wide open for everyone to poke at with their sticks? Am I okay with that? But I am clearly meant to be following the signs. They are plentiful, let me tell you. Once you start noticing them and paying attention to the lessons along the way, the path starts unfolding almost magically before you. So I have to be ready for it, and take the leap of faith that everything will be okay.

I am not saying, you understand, that I believe the entire flood was about me. That would be ridiculous. But it was put into my path to teach me certain lessons. Everyone affected by the flood has their own reason it entered *their* path, and must take their own lessons from it.

For me, this means I need the space and the time out. I have not had a visitor for days and I can feel myself relaxing back into my own space. Hopefully now the words will flow more easily.

Our farm suffered quite extensive damage, and it will take months and money to repair. But if we just keep chipping away at it, one day at a time, it's nothing we can't fix. My outlook on life has changed so much because of you, Sam. Life is too short for negativity and moaning, and I mean literally *too short!* And too fragile. This lifetime here on earth is only the blink of an eye, and we are supposed to be enjoying it.

I have discovered a really powerful connection with the colour yellow. I have never liked it, but since I started my colour therapy course I realise how it gives me joy, like a happy little burst of sunshine when I see it. And that's the key to all of it, I suspect – to awareness, to enlightenment, to awakening. Joy is the key to it all.

Through love and gratitude and positive thoughts I often find myself in a place of complete joy, and that's when the magic happens. The answers to your questions become clear, and it's easier to see the next step.

And for me the next step is the charity.

It's all becoming clear in my head, like a map. Sam has many purposes in our lives, and this is one of them. It's no accident that I got the three children I did. Sam will help his brothers; the love between them is so strong. And the real work is starting now.

During the recent school holidays we couldn't make the time for Jack's daily tutoring. Instead, he helped out on the farm, packing wine and picking flowers and clearing plates at the restaurant. And he has grown up so much. I can see his confidence and pride as he successfully completes each task.

Jack has become a natural yardstick by which we measure people's character. He sometimes carries things to tables at the restaurant, with his pure blue eyes and his earnest stuttering voice. 'Hullo. Is you a customer? Is you want Pinotage or Subnon Blanc?' Those who see the beauty in him immediately take to him, and have a hilarious two-minute conversation that makes their day. Those who seem annoyed, afraid and offended are clearly not the sort of folk we need around. A perfect example of natural selection working its magic.

So now, instead of the more structured tutoring, we are involving him more in the daily running of the farm. Yeah, so maybe he can't write his name yet. Who says that's the most important thing in life anyway?

I believe this physical therapy is different, but effective in a whole new way. But what about school? I have researched all the options, and I believe his current school is best for him. He's at the same school as Alex, in a different class, and I consider it the best option for now. But the school I want my boys to go to doesn't exist in this area – a school that not only tolerates differences but celebrates them.

Children like Jack are different, not less. If someone cries, Jack bursts into tears and won't stop unless the other person is comforted. If I use the last of the Corn Flakes in the morning, Jack will constantly remind me to buy more. The next morning when I bring them out his eyes literally sparkle and his whole face lights up. 'Tank you, Mommy, tank you. Tank you for to buying the Cornflakes!' He is so grateful, so pure and so appreciative.

Tonight he had a fall on his scooter. He grazed his knee, which wasn't a problem until he noticed it twenty minutes later. Then he went into full meltdown, which, unless you've experienced it, is hard to explain. It's about much more than the graze on his knee. It's a rage and a frustration that breaks out of him, over which he has no control. He shouts, 'I sick, I sick! I sad, I sad!' I swear it would break your fucking heart. And Alex is the only one who can fix it. He goes and holds him and says, 'Sorry Jack. I love you, Jack.' Tonight he then arranged a pillow on the couch and positioned his brother's head on it. Then he climbed up next to Jack and lay with his head on the same pillow. And he said, 'You can switch the TV on now, Mom.'

Now they are both cuddled up in the same bed. What a hard and complicated path this second son of mine has to navigate, at all of four years old. But if this is the kind of man he will become, then the lessons have done their work, I guess.

4 December 2013

We drove to Arniston today, a seaside village about an hour from the farm. It's past Cape Agulhas (the southern tip of Africa) and the water is so much warmer than our nearby beaches. The boys, hubby and I lounged in the warm seawater and spent hours jumping in the gentle waves. It was perfect. The sea definitely has a healing effect on me.

I cried quietly in the car all the way there, with my sunglasses on while looking out of the window. Hubby has become somewhat accustomed to these silent tears, and merely reaches over to squeeze my knee in support. Sometimes tears need to flow, and that's now a fact of our lives.

I cried also because of how afraid I've become. Hubby drove carefully and safely as he always has, but every sharp curve, every oncoming car terrifies me. Not for me, but because I have my children with me. I noticed the same thing during the floods. The farm road the next day was fairly treacherous, with deep dongas and running water. But I happily drove along it to the tar road to survey the damage, and rather enjoyed the adventure. When I reached the bottom of the road, I found hubby and the boys, all three of them having navigated the road on a motorbike. They were all bright-eyed and excited, loving it. But I couldn't face the thought of them going back up the road on the bike, so I made some lame excuse to load them up in the bakkie. I strapped them in and started the one-kilometre journey up the road. It was so frightening. What had looked like a stream across the road was suddenly a raging torrent, likely to sweep us away. The dongas were now giant canyons, liable to swallow the entire vehicle. I arrived home white-knuckled and shaking.

It's possible that I have some post-traumatic stress disorder. It would be strange if I didn't. But the only way forward is through. So I keep pushing myself a little further. Yesterday we went on a boat, the four (five) of us. The kids wore their lifejackets and we went slowly. Before we left I asked hubby to go easy on me. I think he understands. But still I clung to them desperately, my mind constantly sending me visions of one of them falling overboard. And when we arrived back on terra firma I thanked God and Sam and all my angels. And I felt very proud.

Little by little, bit by bit, I am fighting my way back to normality. My new normal, that is.

5 December 2013

Today, when we went shopping for groceries, some sorrow finally found its way out of poor Jack. I'm sure it can only be good for him.

We went past the jars of baby food and Jack stopped dead in his tracks and stood staring at the shelves. Then he gently reached out his hand to touch the jars. He used to love feeding Sam. It was his favourite thing, and he was such a proud big brother when he was finally allowed to do it alone.

He turned to me and asked, in his adorable halted speech, 'Mommy. Who. Is. Dis. For?'

'That's for babies,' I said, as gently as I could.

'Is. It. For. Baby. Sam?' he asked, his eyes desperate and confused by the sudden happy memory. 'When he is going to come back?'

So I got down on my knees and I told him again about heaven and angels. And we sat there, in the aisle of the busy supermarket, and we cried. Some parts of this will never get easier.

17 December 2013

Tonight I face a new challenge, and I am nervous. I took a walk in Sam's garden this morning, then lit a candle and had a bath, and prayed to all my angels (even the vacuum-cleaner wielding ones). I opened my laptop so I could watch a recording of our dance routine, and there they were – all three of my boys in a series of photos, playing around with some old sunglasses, Sam on my lap. And I burst into tears, not only because I saw his perfect little face and his soft little cheeks and his beautiful upturned nose, but because immediately and for the first time I noticed what was leaping out at me from the screen.

On the identical, bright red towels Jack and Alex were wearing was the Manchester United slogan, *You'll never walk alone*. The message is so beautiful and full of hope.

This evening is the opening night of the local Stanford show, On Broadway. As previously mentioned, I am dancing in said production. That in itself is totally hilarious, and I shall tell you why.

My whole life I have known I cannot dance. Nor can my siblings – some sort of genetic deficiency. Ever since Sensible Sister first set foot on stage at a ballet recital and brought shame upon the family by forgetting her steps, it's been a long-standing family joke. 'You should've seen her!' my dad would guffaw, slapping his knee. 'Like a little elephant, she was, heading off in the wrong direction.'

'Ha,' we would all chortle. 'Us Yeatses, two left feet, the lot of us!' And so it continued throughout school. Friends loved me dearly, but none would argue that my Captain Co-ord nickname was well earned. Even aerobics proved tricky, my constant confusion posing a danger to everyone around me.

When we started rehearsals five months ago, I expected this experience to be no different. Jami, the clown of the group. I just couldn't get the hang of it and we laughed our asses off, the six women dancing in this particular number. My friend R tied a little ribbon to my shoulder to help me remember which way was left. But somehow, over the course of the past five months, something changed.

I started to really enjoy the dancing and the sense of accomplishment when I mastered another tricky portion of the routine. I began to feel a sense of camaraderie with other cast members and a very real desire not to let them down.

Finally, about a week ago, it happened. I got the entire routine right from start to finish. '*Jeez,* I'm so relieved!' I declared loudly. The choreographer was quite choked up. 'How do you think I feel?' she replied. I swear she was close to weeping.

Suddenly I made a decision. Not only would I do the dance, I would do it as well as I possibly could, and take pride in doing it. I would not do it as a joke, but to disprove once and for all this self-limiting belief that had followed me my whole life.

So this week I went to the mall and bought the tightest pair of black pants I have ever owned. Really badass. Not only am I going to dance this role of sexy murderess; I am going to *own* it. R has done my smoky eye makeup, and she's from the big city so she's done an amazing job. My hair is teased, it's nearly time to get my show gear on and hang around outside the back door of the church hall, chattering nervously and sharing cigarettes with other excited people who have suddenly become my friends.

18 December 2013

That was amazing. What an experience; I am so glad I got to feel that. We all totally killed it, not a step out of place (just about) and the audience *loved* it. Afterwards, in the changing room (or, as we now call it, the life-changing room) we all hugged and laughed and congratulated each other, and the hard work and hours of practise were *totally* worth it.

I made so many new friends of all ages, many of whom I would never have gotten the chance to know. Importantly, it was also a chance to reconnect with my friend R. She and I were pregnant at the same time, she with her second boy and me with our Sam. Sadly, her younger son will always be a physical reminder and yardstick of the life Sam would have had, but that's no reason to avoid a friendship that means a lot to me. If you just face up to it, it's one of those things that gets easier with time.

It's going to take days to get this eye makeup off, though. Our friend G took one look at me. 'Christ, is that R's handiwork? That woman should never be left alone in a room with an eye pencil.'

But clearly the stage calls for slightly less subtlety. I can't wait to do it all over again tonight.

28 December 2013

Christmas. This was a big Christmas, a huge one. On 21 December we hosted a big wedding for hubby's cousin. His two sisters flew in from the UK, his aunts came from Swaziland and Zambia, hubby's father flew in and joined us from Johannesburg, and all manner of family members and cousins rolled into town. My family all came together at Sensible Sister's holiday house in Hermanus.

Thank God for the chaos and mayhem of family. We really needed it. Christmas was hard; it will always be hard. It's like seeing something awesome and thinking, 'I wish the boys could see that.' Christmas is such a happy time, especially for the innocent kids who are oblivious to any of the usual backstage drama. It's such a beautiful and magical thing to see, and for the rest of my life I will think, 'Oh Sam, you would have loved this.'

Only one Christmas you had. Just one. Doesn't seem fair, does it?

Since you left I've been to see many a reader at every opportunity, and each has given me something. A sceptic will tell you that I only select from the readings what I want and can relate to my own circumstances, much as a sceptic will tell you that the purple light around me and the hard pear tree was just refraction, blah, blah. But if they reach me at the perfect time, no matter how, surely these messages are real and relevant? How can that not be true?

I believe we were blessed to have you for that one Christmas.

I believe you stayed for us. One angel reader told me that you were always coming for only a short while, and tried to leave us once before when you were less than a year old. But you had fallen so in love with us all, and could see we weren't yet ready to handle your leaving, so you stayed a while longer.

When Sam was nine months old he had a rather chesty cough for a couple of days, but nothing I thought was cause for alarm. Over-the-counter meds weren't helping, so I took him to the paediatrician just to be safe. She diagnosed him with a dangerous respiratory infection and sent us directly to hospital to check in.

I was panicked, but Sam was grinning all the way, even when they inserted his drip. Hubby and the boys came to see us and drop off clothes and treats, as there was no way I was leaving my baby there to wake up among strange nurses. Two nights and three days we spent there, the two of us snuggled up in a single bed, reading and cuddling. The happiest sick baby I ever saw. I always suspected Sam had organised that alone time for us.

Now I think he might have left us, but changed his mind. He gave himself and us more time, and I am so grateful. If that makes me sound crazy, then so be it. Because it also keeps me sane.

Christmas passed in a blur of wrapping paper, laughter, wine and food. The constant tugging sadness was tempered by the joy being with all that family can bring. On Christmas Eve a candle burnt next to your photo at the table, Sam, and again at lunch on Christmas Day. Merry Christmas, angel. We love you.

1 January 2014

So here we are, at the beginning of a new year. Whatever 2014 holds for us, it cannot compare to the life-altering challenge of 2013. Our old house, the manor house, was rented out by friends over New Year, so we went there to celebrate with them.

Midnight somehow found us next to the pool together, hubby and I – the swimming pool that was your exit point from this world. And we held each other as we said goodbye to that year, and to that place. But never ever, Sam, will we say goodbye to you.

6 January 2014

I am so content right now with this moment. I just had an omelette and am now having a cappuccino and a cigarette, with the sweet sounds of a beautiful singer called Leekie Lee on the speaker behind me. Perfect, except for the one thing always slightly simmering in my heart. To the left I can see Sam's garden blooming in every colour of the rainbow. The butterfly bush at the top by the bench is blooming with magnificent flowers, each like a tiny white butterfly.

We spend time there when we need it. Sometimes I look for hubby and find him somewhere in Sam's garden, pulling out weeds and pottering. I think it's the best form of therapy for him.

This season has been crazy. Our first season in the restaurant, and we were fully booked every day. Everybody raves about this place, and I know the secret of why. Yes, it's a beautiful location, and the food and wine is amazing.

But what they feel here, what they sense, is the love. The love our little team has for each other and for the place we are lucky enough to work in. The love I feel for a place that went from dream to actuality in a year I thought I wouldn't survive. The love we feel for this farm, with all its challenges and imperfections. The love Sam has taught us and shown us.

Jack just arrived here at work. It's about two hundred metres from our new house. He would never come up here alone, but he arrived with a bit of sweat on his brow. 'Who did you come with?' I asked him curiously. 'I was running by myself,' he told me proudly, and then took a sip of my water standing on the table in front of me. I was agog. He never drinks water. Ever. Every day now he does something that amazes me. The new independence he is showing is so heartening. He is going to be just fine, this boy. More than fine.

The school holiday has been a challenge. Jack is growing and learning every day, but still doesn't get the rules of play. If he wants Alex's attention he either whacks him on the head or grabs whatever he's playing with. As one can imagine, this could be fairly annoying if you're an adult, never mind a four-year-old. So understandably Alex occasionally loses it and starts punching.

As a parent, it's a really hard thing to manage. Who do you punish? Many of Jack's behaviours are fairly involuntary. But frankly I can understand Alex's position. I have thought and prayed and meditated. And now I realise the answer is simple. You can't fight it right; you have to love it right. So any such behaviour is followed by forced hugs and a little mantra. 'We are brothers and we...' I start, '...love each other,' they finish.

And every day the love between them grows. Yesterday Alex was crying, because another boy had been mean to him, and Jack ran over and just held him. And Alex allowed himself to be held by his big brother. Last night Jack fell asleep on the couch, and when I looked up, Alex was busy covering him with a blanket. Very carefully, so as not to wake him. Making sure his feet were covered, and that the blanket was tucked snugly around him. He looked up, saw me watching and smiled. 'Jack fell asleep,' he told me by way of explanation. My heart nearly burst with love.

Alex has figured out his own way. He is the only one who can calm Jack down sometimes when he's crying and make him laugh by being silly. And he has special hidey-holes around the house and restaurant where he sits and plays when he can't handle any interruptions.

Life will be fine, and everything will work out just as it must.

School starts next week, with Alex still in little class and Jack headed for Grade R. He's still in a mainstream school, but can only stay on if we hire a full time facilitator to accompany him to class. Jack can learn anything, I'm sure of it, but not in the same way as everyone else. With the teacher in front of the class talking, I think all he hears is, 'Waa, waa, waa.' But if you sit next to him and show him something, he is so keen, so desperate to learn.

It hasn't been an easy decision to make as parents. Is it the right thing, trying so hard to mainstream Jack? I've been to see all the special needs schools in the area, and none of them seems right for Jack. Yet the last thing I want is for Jack to be in a mainstream school and always feel 'less than'. Would it be better to go the special needs route where he can shine in class?

We have to trust our intuition on this. It's too soon to put Jack in a box (if you'll excuse the pun), to separate him from his brother and mainstream society. Who knows what he's capable of? From this year on, the boys' nanny V will accompany Jack to school and facilitate his learning. She's known him forever; she understands how special his nature is. And I can't wait to see how high our boy can fly.

10 January 2014

I have had an epiphany. An honest-to-God light has suddenly gone on in my head, and I'm almost giddy with excitement. I have asked for signs and followed them, and they have led me to the next step. On 10 February 2014 I will stop smoking.

If you knew me personally you would be completely agog. It's the one thing I have stubbornly refused to discuss. I am a smoker. Not a namby-pamby, sometimes-when-I've-been-drinking-shooters kind of smoker. I'm a wake-in-the-night-for-a-ciggie and hack-your-lungs-up-every-morning kind of smoker. I smoke first thing in the morning, I smoke when I'm hiking and I'll drive any distance if I'm caught without cigarettes. Recently, during the floods, I risked life and limb rather than be without them.

Hubby has stopped a few times with apparent ease. I know he would never have started again if it wasn't for my refusal to consider joining him. Once he basically tried to force me, which didn't end well, as such things seldom do. It ended in a blowout after he found me smoking around the corner at the pub. So mature, so dignified. It's a package deal, I've reminded him often. It's me and the cigarettes, and that's what he signed up for.

I've tried the books. I've tried hypnosis. I've tried the electronic cigarette. But nothing could make me *want* to stop. I smoked throughout, making light of it and laughing uproariously with my friends over a glass of wine. 'If there's one thing I'm not, it's a quitter,' I would tell them to laugh off this weakness.

I'll stop when I'm ready, I have always said. But inside I have whispered to myself, 'You'll never be ready. You're Jami the smoker, cigarette in hand. If you remove it from the picture, you'll never be the same person.'

It's just another self-limiting belief then, isn't it? If I can get through losing Sam without falling apart, why the hell do I think I'm not strong enough to stop smoking? Bollocks to that. It's frigging personal now, between me and the cigarettes. And I will win.

All my cards have been telling me to detox and take better care of my body. An article crossed my path about angels helping you to overcome addictions, and asking them to help you. Conversations around the topic kept coming up. But still I didn't really let it sink in, fearful at the thought of giving up my biggest crutch.

Last night I went to visit Arty Sister, and found her preparing homemade corn bread. When she turned it out of the loaf tin, it flopped itself messily on the counter in the shape of an omelette. After killing ourselves laughing, and lovingly serving it to the children as corn frittata, we retired outside to chat, drink tea and smoke.

And man, did we smoke. When we're together we get into some kind of smoking frenzy, lighting one after another, as if somehow the next sentence will be ruined without a cigarette in hand while telling or hearing it. We spoke and we laughed and we smoked, and it was completely awesome. We spoke about our history, our family, our beliefs and our challenges. But we didn't speak about smoking.

I then went to Sensible Sister's house, where we sat outside and drank red wine, and I smoked cigarette after cigarette as we solved all the problems of the world together. No, really, I do think we solved a couple of things, but I'm sure those will come up later.

This morning I woke up and had one cigarette, carefully

and lovingly saved from the night before. I had coffee and that cigarette and then there I was... cigaretteless. My worst nightmare. By 8 am I had no choice. Instead of lounging about in my pyjamas having tea and chats, I had to get dressed and get to the shops. On the way there I had a coughing fit that made my eyes water. So instead of driving directly to the shop, I drove to a nearby beach to think and be still.

I sat in the car for ten minutes and looked at the big, beautiful sea. And I realised. This is fucking ridiculous. How can I allow something, anything, to hold so much power over me?

I am going to use my own method, cobbled together from various books I have read and courses I have attended. My key tools will be prayer, meditation and affirmations. This morning I did go to the shop and buy the cigarettes, but I bought a different brand. This has two advantages: they taste revolting, and my brand loyalty is now removed from the equation.

I will continue to smoke as much as I feel I need to over the next month, as long as I buy cheap and nasty cigarettes. And every day I will pray and meditate and ask for Sam's help to make this an easy and joyful transition from smoker to non-smoker.

And on 10 February, two days after the anniversary I am dreading the most, I will stop in honour of my darling boy, and of what he has taught me and the strength I know he has given me. I will do this for my family.

I have been doing my affirmations today. Looking myself square in the eye and repeating, 'I cannot wait to be a joyful non-smoker. I will be healthy and my family will be healthy. I will be free and I will still be me'.

I have done a vision board of what my life will look like as a non-smoker, all white teeth and sporty outdoor adventure. And when I was doing it I just cracked up, because I remembered when my mother and I attended a course together to stop smoking. We proudly did our vision boards at home and whipped them out when we got to class. She was making noises of approval while eyeing mine, and then I spotted something suspicious. 'What's this?' I enquired. 'A cruise liner, Jami. I'd like to go on a cruise.' I had to point out the peculiar angle of the ship's deck and the many tiny figures waving frantically in the surrounding ocean before she would admit that she'd accidentally cut out a picture of the Titanic.

And that's my mom, for you. Ditzy in the most adorable way. Can never find her things, and always mildly frazzled. But everyone loves my mom. She is mostly soft and kind, but God knows, if you need it, that woman can be strong and terrifying. Known among a generation of teenage boys as The Dragon Lady but adored by them all, who still speak about her legendary meals. With three daughters in high school at the same time, our home was never short of visitors. We brought girlfriends from the hostel who had come to spend the holiday in Hermanus, and with them came a steady stream of teenage male suitors. Shaking off the morning's beach sand, they were welcomed by day with huge pies and trays of lasagne. But at night they would cower in the garden as the lights snapped on and my mother's silhouette appeared in the doorway. 'I know you're there, all of you! I've taken your license plate numbers and I'm calling your parents!' Her shouts would cause a flurry of hormone-addled boys to retreat.

But the real Carol is soft, kind and funny. My wedding day pretty much sums her up. The minister was late and Mom had worked herself into quite a tither. Flustered and fidgety, she absentmindedly spritzed behind her ears with the small bottle of perfume she carried in her handbag. As The Brother walked me down the aisle, we noticed my mother and sisters sitting together with tears pouring down their faces, in a rather touching display of emotion. Only later did we hear that our sisters had just finished beating our mother around the head. Alas, she'd mistaken her cigarette lighter for her perfume and accidentally set her hairspray alight.

It's one of my favourite stories, but God, there are many. Each one only serves to illustrate her lovely uniqueness, and reminds me that it's people's little idiosyncrasies that make them special. So when I do something particularly scatty (which is fairly often), and hubby looks at me in despair, I simply tell him haughtily, 'I can't help it. It's genetic,' and walk away proudly.

12 January 2014

A h, that feels better. Back to writing with a pen in the black
Moleskin journal that saw the start of the story. One of my
favourite people, my friend K, brought it to me when Sam left.
It was sent by her mother, a very important influence on my love
of words. She was an English professor of mine, and someone
who truly believed in my writing. And the words are flowing
easily again.

I've been a bit stuck. Feeling rushed by no-one other than
myself, I've been writing straight onto my laptop to save time.
I have asked the words to flow and asked for signs and help.
This morning I opened my laptop to write and found the screen
cracked and blank, refusing to flicker into life. For a minute I
was distraught. With us away on holiday, how would I write?
Then I remembered that I'd brought along my journal, in case
I needed to check anything. 'Duh, you idiot,' I stopped just
short of slapping my forehead with an open palm. It's a *sign*,
obviously. I beetled off to get my journal, picked up a pen and
haven't stopped scribbling.

We are away at one of my all-time favourite places for a hard-
earned, much-needed, God-this-feels-good family holiday. The
place is called Mabalingwe, a game farm north of Johannesburg
in the African bush, with peace and quiet and wild animals. I
feel so at home here. We had a totally amazing sign from Sam
on the way here.

Yesterday I posted this as my Facebook status:

Finally, our little family gets a proper holiday. Literally thousands of butterflies on our way here, like swarms. Hard to avoid on the highway. Never seen anything like it. Very powerful soul on holiday with us!

This morning I opened my computer to find so many comments on it, and a number of news site links posted to my wall, including this one from News24:

Butterfly migration comes to Johannesburg
Johannesburg – Swarms of white butterflies have descended on Johannesburg during their annual migration from South Africa's west coast to Madagascar, lepidopterist Earle Whiteley said on Saturday. Whiteley, a director of Conservation of Butterflies in SA, said that the spectacle was an annual event, but that the clouds of Belenois aurota, commonly known as brown veined white butterflies, did not always follow exactly the same route. 'They start hatching along the entire coast from Cape Town towards Namibia, then migrate inland in a north-easterly direction.' Whiteley said that the initial batch of butterflies were joined by more and more along their migratory route, over the Eastern Cape, which had now reached Gauteng. The butterflies would then head toward Mozambique before crossing the sea to Madagascar. 'As they are going further north, some die and more join. Eventually, there are massive clouds of butterflies, reaching up to a kilometre into the air.' Along the route, the female butterflies laid eggs, which would begin the life cycle of the next generation. The timing of the migration was dependant on weather conditions, but usually ran from late November to mid-February. The brown veined white butterflies were often joined by other butterflies of the same Pieridae family, which had shades of yellow or orange in their colouration. The butterflies travelled from sunrise to dusk and needed to replenish themselves

with nectar every 20 minutes or risk dying from dehydration. They favoured long grass and were particularly attracted to grass nectar, Whiteley said. The butterflies roost overnight, and it was possible to tell whether a butterfly was awake or asleep by looking at their feelers. 'If the feelers are touching, then they are sleeping.' Whiteley was working towards establishing the Gauteng Butterfly Sanctuary, which is expected to open in December.[1]

Coincidence? Seriously? I would have given anything to see a butterfly migration, but I didn't even know they happened in South Africa. I thought you had to go to South America somewhere. Quite by surprise, the butterflies arrive at our route at the same time as we do, and accompany us all the way to our destination. Coincidence, my ass.

It was hot when we arrived at Mabalingwe yesterday, the kind of thick, heavy heat that feels like a blanket around you.

The kids stripped off and headed straight for the pool on the elevated stoep of the house overlooking nothing but vast African bush. We settled at the big wooden table and watched a thunderstorm pull in.

It's the most exhilarating thing, a Highveld storm. First an eerie silence descends and the heat grows even more oppressive. Suddenly the sound of thousands of birds and the buzzing of cicadas rises up from the dense canopy of green. Then we watch the rain approach, accompanied by the deep rumble of thunder and great forks of lightning tearing the sky. Glass of wine in hand, my family with me, all I could think was, 'Wow. How crazy blessed am I?'

This powerful spiritual experience was naturally punctured by cries of, '*Mommy*, come and wipe my *bum*,' and 'Alex did smack me,' and 'Mommy, Mommy, Mommy, I want juice!' But even for that, especially for that, I am grateful.

Being completely broken and facing the depth of true pain has

1 www.news24.com/Southafrica/news/butterfly-migration-comes-to-johannes-burg-20140112

had the effect of exponentially increasing my capacity for joy. And I have discovered that, for me, the key to it all is gratitude.

I am so, so grateful that I had you, Sam, however briefly. The pain is still there, of course, and the tears flow along their well-worn tracks as I write. I am so grateful that I have your brothers. I am grateful for my kind, loving, often frigging annoying hubby, and for all my family and friends. I am grateful for my strong limbs, this cup of coffee, this time alone, and the outside shower I intend to have in a few minutes. Everyone has something to be grateful for, and if you focus on that rather than the things you don't have, your life will change.

I intend to live joyfully this year; to dance and sing, celebrate all the good in my life and be completely true to myself.

I have worked a lot this last year on boundaries, and man, has it felt good. I do not intend to take shit from anyone this year, and that includes myself. No more self-flagellating because of all the things I am not, but celebrating what I am instead. So what if I'm a bit scatty and my car is always a mess? I have plenty of other good points, and I'll focus on those instead.

8:30 pm

A beautiful day with my children. They amaze me, all three of them. I am so aware of Sam's presence here, and so are the kids. Clouds of white butterflies continue to float out of the long grass as we drive past, and Alex says, 'We're so lucky. Baby Sam is sending us lots of messages'. And he is.

I came out by myself onto the stoep earlier and prayed, as I always do, to God and Sam and my angels. I need to see things clearly now, to maintain a balance and trust the flow. Work is getting busier daily, as everything suddenly falls into place. The restaurant is packed with people, the wine is flying out of the cellar. Sam, you continue to amaze me.

But we have such an awesome team now, each one amazing in their respective roles. This year I must shift my focus to my family and to myself.

14 January 2014

Another amazing day of holiday. Jack has just finished packing the dishes away and is now busy vacuuming in the nude. Not happy unless he has a job, a purpose, this boy. So earnest as he carefully removed each one, talking all the time to himself in a little singsong voice. 'Diiss iss de dishes. I must pack dem *awaaaay*.' Hanging each piece of cutlery on the stand in its correct position – all those matching games paying off. Every day he pushes himself that little bit further and grows more confident. I can't watch him put the plates away, so scared am I that he'll break one. Couldn't give a toss about the plate, of course; it's watching his meltdown, his own heartbreak, that's the hard bit. As he stretches himself, he is also bound to flirt with failure at times. But for Jack, every mistake he makes is a disaster, and he freaks out, berating himself, smacking himself on the head and making his wailing sound. And, ooh, that's tough to watch. But this time he didn't drop a single plate, and he's beaming from ear to ear. I am so proud of him.

Alex is watching cartoons on the couch with a cup of hot chocolate. He is the strong one, the one I know will lead and always be okay.

Hubby is lying in the hammock reading. It's a pretty perfect moment.

Hubby took the boys out for a game drive this afternoon. They had a fantastic time and Alex can't stop looking at the photo he took of the rhinos they saw, completely astounded that such an animal exists. Being here alone on this wooden deck overlooking the bush was magical. I was making myself a cup of tea when I heard a crack of thunder. I came out to sit under the thatch with my tea and think. I made some decisions about the book, and suddenly it seemed more possible, more real.

It was still sweltering hot when the big, plump raindrops started, and I put down my tea and stepped out from under the thatch. As the rain soaked me I felt cleansed, and I cried great big tears of grief and gratitude.

18 January 2014

Today we are heading home from our holiday. It's always nice to go away, but also great to go home. I woke up excited to see everyone back home, and for a few blissfully confused seconds I thought, 'Yay, I'll get to see Sam'. Then the heart-breaking realisation… you are not there. The pain of losing you is as raw as it always will be.

21 January 2014

I clicked on a link on Facebook, and read something beautiful by a woman named Julie Daley. It's called 'Allow the Dark to Grow You', and it really spoke to me. But the last few lines just broke me.

> Don't fear the dark. It is rich with nutrients, rich with soul food.
> Yes, it will strip you away; yes, you will be transformed; yes,
> you will be reborn –
> If you allow the dark to grow you.
> If you allow the dark to grow you,
> You will bring back to life all that you pretended to put to death;
> And all that you've pretended is life and alive, will die.

It came over me out of nowhere. Like a tsunami I could feel the wall of grief approaching before it physically slammed me. I ran to the only place that felt safe, my dressing room where Sam's little area of remembrance is. And, for the first time, I picked up his ashes and held them against me as I knelt and released the great heaving sobs from my heart.

Now I feel better. It's natural for me to feel that grief, but I can't afford to live in that place, nor dwell there too long in case I can't find my way back. For where would that leave us all?

I sat down and messaged my friend and teacher M. I'm going to see her this afternoon and I'm beside myself with excitement.

23 January 2014

I am lying writing in your garden, Sam. The grass has finally grown enough on one level for me to laze around on. The sun is shining, the birds are chirping. And, of course, there are butterflies. Friends brought plants they knew would attract butterflies and plants to support the life cycle of butterflies. With 8 February approaching, I have asked friends to come to your garden on the day and to bring something to plant. This garden gets more magnificent by the day, and I hope that other people will find peace here just as I do.

Is it really that long already? A whole year without you? You would have been two and half years old now. A difficult age, but I know you would have been kind and lovely and adorable. We were at a restaurant the other day where a boy of about two was screaming his head off. 'Hmm,' said Alex disapprovingly, 'Baby Sam never screamed like that. He was a good boy.' How beautiful that he can speak of Sam. And how desperately, heartbreakingly sad.

In this last year we have lost too many people. It has been a year of memorials. Our dear friend PJ lost to cancer. My friend D's mother and also D lost to cancer. Our friend M killed in an airplane accident in the prime of his life, leaving a wife and two young kids. The kind soul N who was supposed to appear in 'On Broadway' with us has also gone. For each of them I have placed a stone in Sam's garden with their name on and a message. I hope that in future others can do the same. At the top of the garden is what the kids call the Wishing Barrel. You write a wish or a letter and post it in the barrel and it will reach heaven. When the barrel is full all the messages will be composted and put back into the garden.

Where I sit now on this bench in the shade of a tree looking out over the whole garden, I can see and feel the love. There are hundreds of plants and flowers, pottery bunnies, chunks of rose quartz and a rusty metal butterfly. Each was given with pure, unconditional love.

It is a powerful place.

Beyond that I see the restaurant on the dam where the staff are scurrying around preparing for another busy day. There are vineyards to my left and olive trees to my right. I feel incredibly blessed.

People who come here love this place and keep coming back. I laughed with chef B the other day when I saw her putting beautiful, edible nasturtiums from Sam's garden into the salads. 'No wonder they love this place,' I told her. 'You're feeding them pure love!'

My friend M is so wise, I am glad I went to see her. I am so worried about the Oprah magazine article coming out. It feels like the point of no return on this new leg of the journey. I worry about how this will change our lives, about whether I am up to it, that the book will not be well received, that I will look poncy or full of myself, or like I think I know all the answers. I don't. I'm just busy figuring it all out myself.

But in many wise ways, M managed to remind me and reassure me that this is my path. And yours, Sam. And our family's. That there really is no choice but to follow it. Now is the time for courage.

I just looked up at the sky and there, clear as a bell, was a rhino. I never used to see shapes in the clouds, despite my best efforts. I used to spend ages lying on the grass trying. But nothing, absolutely nada. The other day I was sitting on the stoep of my friends N and K's awesome new farmhouse, and there in the clouds was written the word Jami. Even K was dumbstruck, and you know how sceptical most men are. And as the three of us watched, the clouds shifted and formed the word Sam. I shit you not; you can ask them.

For tonight, I have a special bottle of oil to bath in. Coral and olive green, self-esteem and hope for the future. That should keep me strong.

Someone is coming to see me now regarding the Butterfly Foundation. People who can help and who want to help and who have the skills to help keep on crossing my path. This must be my focus now.

We have raised enough to fund our first project – to save a little boy's eyesight. Locally he was told one eye would have to be removed and he was almost certain to lose sight in the other. We took him to a specialist who feels confident that the eyesight in the left eye can be restored by treating the infection, and that there's a chance we can restore sight in the right eye too.

So we have raised the necessary funds and booked another appointment for March. Already, little Endenako is so excited and proud of the glasses that have helped his vision so much. He is all smiles, and when he comes to play, he first lovingly removes his glasses and gently wraps them before packing them away in their case.

It's beautiful. I think this is going to be huge, Sam, and bring us so much joy. I think an integral part of finding joy and fulfilment in your own life is finding a way to give back.

My friend C has done a logo, and I have been in contact with a local charity I totally admire. Until we are able to register our own NPO, we will operate under the umbrella of Food 4 Thought Community projects, with Butterfly Foundation funds collected and managed by a separate committee.

The long-term plan, as far off as it may seem, must be written down for it all to start falling into place. We would like to buy a property where we could start a therapy centre for children with special needs, as there is nothing like that here in our rural area. In fact, I would like it to be a farm. Eventually this could lead to a school. A properly inclusive, forward-thinking school with a variety of traditional therapies and more esoteric, complimentary therapies to fully support children like Jack, who currently don't seem to quite fit.

And with that, with Sam behind the charity that will help his brother and others like him, another part of the puzzle falls into place.

31 January 2014

Ihave had the most difficult week since you left, Sam. It's coming up to one year and emotions are running high. I am tired, post-season. So is hubby, and he is gearing up to start harvest next week. We need to be strong to give it our all, yet life doesn't always respect our need to focus on work.

I live in a tiny village where people know our family and our story. Because of Jack's special needs, the local school is not the best place for him, although they did try to accommodate him. I have found what I consider to be the best school for my children, but it's not in the local village where we're loved and protected.

I take them both to school in Hermanus, twenty minutes' drive away. I love the time we spend together in the car, so the driving isn't really the problem. But it's a bigger town, and most people there have a very warped, speculative version of our tragedy. If you don't know me, I'm the strange creature who lost her child (an irresponsible mother, obviously, because my only real responsibility is to keep my children alive, and I have failed). I am an alien creature and treated as such. But you, reading this, are you a parent too? How can you judge me? Have you any idea how cruel that is?

It is partly that people find it difficult to approach me. They don't feel they can mention Sam, yet don't know how to speak to me without mentioning him. Sensible Sister recently went out to dinner with me. She saw how people's faces changed when

I walked in, the sudden silence and the whispering. '*Jesus*,' she said in a sympathetic whisper, 'how do you handle this? It's like being some kind of anti-celebrity'.

Anyway, one of my great friends reported to me after a playdate that there was speculation about Sam's drowning, how it happened and, more importantly, whose fault it was.

The judgement sent me back into the dangerous world of self-blame, and I came up against a wall of despair. I know this feeling. It's a wall you can't climb over or burrow under. You have to push directly through, brick by painful brick.

So I 'opossumed' myself and sobbed, prayed and meditated my way through it. I tried to go to work yesterday, and the girls, God love 'em, took one look at me and sent me away. Some girl wine time was their recommendation. So I sobbed my way to my mother's house, where she poured me some wine, tried to force feed me and rubbed some sort of healing plant (very comforting) onto the pimple on my cheek. I phoned my friend N, and she quickly locked up her office and came to me. And we cried and laughed and drank wine as I spoke about how I was feeling. 'Screw them,' they declared, 'they don't even know you.' And most importantly, they repeated, 'It wasn't your fault. You're not to blame.'

I came home feeling a bit lighter, and spent a pleasant evening at home with hubby, bathing the boys and just being mommy. This morning I woke up and waited for the heavy feeling to descend on me. And it wasn't there. I leapt out of bed and danced a joyful jig. 'I've got my *happy* back! Thank you, Sam!'

1 February 2014

And so we have entered the month of February. The shortest month of the year, but for the rest of my life, I suspect, it will be the longest. It's all so familiar – the long, sweltering afternoons, the flurry of activity on the farm as we prepare for the grape harvest – yet completely and entirely different. Last year you were here with us, Sam; this year you are not. You took up so little physical space, but your leaving has left a gap that is impossible to measure. Eighty-seven centimetres tall, you were. I know, because your dad recorded all the heights of you boys on the wall in our old house over the years, then measured and redrew them on the wall of our new home. And there it is, a little line marked with an S, taken the month before you left. The little line drawn over your beautiful, thick, dark hair. Underneath that was a perfect body – all muscle, blue eyes, soft skin and a toothy grin. And that space, that eighty-seven centimetres, is as big as the entire universe.

This month I will become a non-smoker. I am both scared and excited.

2 February 2014

The bike. It's like a stab in my heart every time I see it. Seeing it standing there unused, fading and rusting, my nanny V asked yesterday if she could buy it for her son. She doesn't realise – no-one does – that getting rid of this bicycle would be like giving up, and I just fucking can't. As I sit here tonight, hubby is busy adjusting the seat, as if making it higher will somehow give Jack the ability to pedal.

He just can't. He wants to so very badly; I can see it in the focused look in his eyes and in the set of his mouth.

Here we go. The seat has been raised. And hubby is crawling behind him, showing Jack the motion. 'This foot goes down, see? And this one comes up.' But there he sits, stationary. Saying to himself, 'Foot over, foot over.' And I sit and cry behind my sunglasses, and I know. 'This is okay. This is who you are, Jack, and (bicycle riding later or never) you are perfect.'

4 February 2014

This week is very hard. I am doing okay but I keep my sunglasses on in public. The tears regularly take me by surprise, in the supermarket or while dropping the boys at school.

That is to be expected, I suppose. Sam is sending us all the strength he can, that I know. My friend M just called me. 'Did you see all the butterflies on the way to Hermanus?' she asked incredulously. Oh indeed I did. So many people have commented on it today through Facebook and sms.

I drove the boys to school this morning, and the butterflies weren't around yet. Then I went for a walk along the sea, and sat down on a rock and cried and prayed. (Please Sam, tell me you weren't scared, my baby boy. Let me know and make me strong.)

Then I had to go to the stationery shop to get a few things. Flip files, coloured card and ink cartridges. The flip files there, naturally, are created by a company called Butterfly. Likewise the coloured card. And funnily, I never before noticed that HP cartridges have butterflies on their packaging.

Then on the way home, swarms of beautiful white winged messages, and I can't help but smile. 'Show off!' I think, with utmost love and awe. I can almost hear his giggle.

5 February 2014

I have had another insight this week, which could be pretty important going forwards. Hubby and I had words, and they were not friendly ones. At the root of it all, regardless of what arbitrary incident triggered it, was money.

It's all too often the case, isn't it, for most of us? People who have too much fight about it, people who have too little fight about it, as do people somewhere in between. It's horrendous. I have no desire to waste my life fighting about money. It's just a means to an end. So why am I letting it happen?

It was a humdinger of a fight, and hubby and I took a two-night break from each other, which is unheard of. I used the days to think, to walk by the sea and meditate on the rocks. (Please note, this sounds more advanced and enlightened than it actually is. I am still having lots of trouble with visualisation and with complete stillness. But I like to think that just sitting in silence for twenty minutes, when I can, will be enough to get me there eventually.)

I thought about money, about how I felt about it and how I treat it. I thought deeply to recall my earliest memories about money.

I must have been four or five years old when money went missing from a piggy bank in the household, which was destined for my brother. For whatever reason, suspicion fell on me. I denied it, but eventually, from sheer confusion at the accusation, I 'confessed' and was sent to my room. (Remembering this, I have since confirmed my suspicion that Arty Sister was behind the wicked deed. She shows little remorse, and will only comment that the feathery scarf she purchased with the money brought her great joy.)

Jokes aside, I then wondered why this memory stood out, and how it influenced my current relationship with money. Numerous times thereafter I remember being caught for minor pilfering. I suspect deep down I felt that if they were going to blame me for stealing, I may as well bloody steal. Luckily I grew out of the pilfering by about thirteen, but something stayed behind like a stain on my psyche.

Then it hit me. That's exactly how I behave with money. I'm still just that naughty child who never earned it, doesn't deserve it and somehow feels dirty for having it. I spend recklessly sometimes, especially when pissed off. It makes me feel good to get rid of the filthy lucre. Then I hide the spending from my husband like a naughty little child, and so he treats me like one. And then I just see red.

Ha! What a discovery! It's not *all* my fault, of course; he has his own money issues which he frigging better work on. But I am taking back my power. There will be no more wrinkled slips at the bottom of my bag between the bits of tissues and cigarettes.

Gone is the tatty old wallet I've had for about six years that looks like a cat chewed it. I emptied it and gave all the slips to T at the office to file, and then went to Hermanus and bought myself a beautiful new wallet, exactly the colour of Sam. And I am ready to receive abundance in all its forms. Because I deserve it.

Money is not bad, you see. Nor is it good. It's just pieces of paper that we need to exchange to retain order in the world. The value we give it is up to us. But, as with anything, you'll never reach a place of abundance if you don't respect and appreciate what you already have.

6 February 2014

Last night, at this time when I needed it most, Sam came to me. Once before I have seen the back of him, and once I awoke with a memory of having seen his smiling face. But this time he came to me. I dreamt that I was sitting on the side of my bed, and something touched my knee. I looked down and there you were, just as perfect as I remembered. I dropped to my knees, and we reached for each other and held on tight, right there on the floor of our lovely bedroom in our new home. And we stayed like that for a second, and for a lifetime.

I woke up crying tears of both sorrow and joy. And I felt more energised than I have in months. We can move forward, Sam. We can be a happy family, and moving forward doesn't mean leaving you behind. No matter where life takes us, you will be there.

8 February 2014

So here it is. The day has dawned, the day that has loomed threateningly before me like an enormous, gaping chasm. How deep will it be, how wide, how dark? Will I be able to find my way out? Do I still have the strength left in me for another test, another climb?

It's the completion of a full cycle, and the last of the firsts. The first birthday, the first Christmas, the first of everything. At the end of today I will have felt them all, and know that I can survive them.

Yesterday evening was hard. A tight knot of dread in my stomach about what was to come. It was also the kids' Sports Day, which I love and wouldn't miss for the world.

First came the intro races, the two- to three-year-olds with their podgy little legs tripping over each other and heading off in the wrong direction. I couldn't help but picture you with them, Sam. You would have so kicked ass. I could picture you running towards me, grinning and holding out your arms. Behind my sunglasses my heart was bleeding.

Then it was Alex's turn, and a measure of joy returned. The crack in my heart shrank to its normal, bearable size. It was an egg and spoon race, and although Alex finished right at the back, he was by no means last. He was the only kid who was completely focused and took it absolutely seriously. Other children were running holding the egg, or dropped it and just kept going. But Alex moved steadily behind them, slowly and carefully, and as he crossed the line I knew in my heart that he had won that race. So did he, as he raced over excitedly to give me a high five. He is going to be just fine, that little boy, as long as we keep dissolving his anger with love.

Then it was Jack's turn. Hubby and I looked at each other with some concern when we realised it was a sack race. 'Erm,' I said nervously to the nearest teacher, 'has he tried this before?' I've been in this game for nearly seven years now, and my mommy danger radar was conjuring pictures of a bloody nose.

The race kicked off. Jack put all his energy into jumping and didn't fall over. However, he jumped up and down mostly in the same place, so progress was painfully slow. The other children had already finished when a teacher approached me. 'Maybe you'd better meet him halfway.' She didn't have to ask twice. It had taken superhuman strength to stop myself running to him in the first place.

I went halfway up the field, put out my arms and called his name. And I saw that determination in his eyes, and the joy that followed when he eventually reached me. All the parents and children clapped and cheered for this brave and wonderful boy, and I saw how his chest puffed out with pride.

He's going to be just fine, this boy.

Sheila the dog never did come home, sadly. The boys are most annoyed at her for finding a boyfriend, marrying him and eloping to live in the mountains. Just before Christmas this year we got a new dog, a mixed breed that appears to be mostly Jack Russell. The boys chose her from Animal Welfare, because she could jump the highest, and Alex was delighted by this 'dog that can jump like a frog', whom they named Twinkletoes Mc Boing Boing, or Twinkle for short. She was utterly mute for her first three months with us. Then last week she leapt up and barked, and hubby and I looked at each other in delight. She has finally found her voice.

Twinkle spends her evenings cuddling with Jack and her days in the passenger seat of hubby's bakkie, or occasionally on his motorbike. I'm not sure who loves her more.

Hubby is working hard, but loving every minute of it. He can still be *very* annoying, and occasionally grumpy. We still argue about silly stuff, and sometimes about big stuff. All we can do is to keep reminding ourselves how lucky we are and keep loving each other. I think that man is going to be okay.

Last night I came home from Sports Day and lit a new candle, a beautiful turquoise one. I took a photo and put it on Facebook and asked our friends to light a candle for Sam. I thought of you looking down, Sam, and seeing all the little lights with your name on them flickering all over the world. You will see once again how many lives you touched and how very loved you are.

I woke up this morning to a Facebook page filled with pictures of candles lit for you all over the world. God, Sam, you are such a special and powerful soul. We are so lucky and grateful to have you in our lives.

This morning has not been pretty. There have been great big heaving sobs as the fire of physical grief tore through my body. But now I sit here with a cup of tea and I can hear the birds singing again. I smile tentatively. I think that may be the worst of it. I hope so.

Hubby and Jack have gone to the local co-op to choose some plants, and then we will take the boys to work in Sam's garden. Some dear friends will join us during the course of the day, some okay-to-sob-in-front-of friends. Your garden is looking magnificent, my boy. And we absolutely feel you there.

This year, I intend to take care of myself and my family, physically as well as mentally. I will show my poor hard-done-by body some much-needed respect for all the crap I have put it through these last thirty-nine years.

I love my walking and running, and I intend to make time for it. The other day I made a bulgur wheat salad, for Christ's sake, and the family actually ate it. I have also learnt the correct pronunciation of quinoa and how to prepare it.

I used my Colour Mirrors deck today, and this is the card I pulled.

Black Phoenix

Rebirth

Out of the darkness comes the light. Without the dark you would not know that light exists. During our search for the meaning of our lives we get to experience our shadow, darker aspects. At times, we will feel that we are being consumed by events that we seem to have no control over, taking us on a roller coaster ride.

Black teaches us that we have to completely strip away all fear, all beliefs that keep us small and powerless, and embrace ourselves as light.

The process of black can leave us feeling naked, vulnerable and helpless – with good reason. When you are reborn, you are like a new baby and have to grow up in the level of awareness you were birthed into. This new level is a space where you can start afresh, like a phoenix rising out of the ashes, more powerful and beautiful than before. Now is a good time to 'allow in' family support and nurturing for every aspect of your life. Soon you will feel stronger and grow into a spiritual adult that consciously creates the most perfect reality.

On Monday, two things will happen. First, I will wake up a non-smoker. I have asked Sam and the angels to help me, and I know they will.

Second, I will leave for a four-night retreat at a most beautiful spiritual place in McGregor, a village a couple of hours drive away. There I will pray and meditate my way through this challenge, and make myself stronger than the cigarettes.

This book will finish today, and I will spend next week typing it up to send to the publishers the following week. On 17 February, The Oprah magazine will be on the shelves, and there will be no turning back. It's scary; of course, it is. If I thought it was hard putting our family out there before, it was nothing compared to this. But this is my commitment to you, my boy. I have promised to follow the signs to my true path, the reason and purpose for all of this, and it is a promise I cannot and will not break. It's time to trust the flow.

And what about me? Am I going to be okay? You know what, Sam? With you by my side I think I'm going to be just fine. We both are.

THE END
(and the beginning)

Acknowledgements

I would like to thank so many people, and I am so scared that I will forget someone. But firstly, thanks to Sam for living with us. To hubby and the boys for their strength and bravery. My mother for being her beautiful unique self, my sisters and brother for the tears and the laughter. My father for instilling in me a love of words and a sense of humour. Hubby's family for the love and support in so many ways... thank you Cathryn, Peter, Andrew, Lynn, Ursula, Caroline and all the extended bunch. The team and my partners at Stanford Hills for supporting my dream. My most amazing friends for doing my nails, making me tea, bringing me ciggies, holding me when I cried, pouring wine when I need it and for loving our family. You really do know who you are. Special mention must be made of darling friend K who has supported my writing always and did the first bit of editing on this book. To the community of Stanford and the wider Overberg region, we are blessed to live among such wonderful people. To everyone at Jacana Media who heard and understood the message.

Thank you to each and every person who has written to us, who has commented on my blog, who has sent us butterfly gifts. Every one of your supportive comments and stories has helped me to trust this journey. Thanks to the various teachers along my life path, those I have met and those I have yet to encounter.

Namaste.